A STRANGER AT YOUR DOOR

"Here I am standing at the door and knocking. If anyone listens to My call and opens the door, I will come in to him. . . ."

The Apocalypse, 3:20

A Stranger
at Your Door

JOHN J. POWELL, S.J.

THE BRUCE PUBLISHING COMPANY
MILWAUKEE

IMPRIMI POTEST:

    WILLIAM J. SCHMIDT, S.J.
    Praepositus Provincialis

NIHIL OBSTAT:

    JOANNES A. SCHULIEN, S.T.D.
    Censor librorum

IMPRIMATUR:

    ✠ ALBERTUS G. MEYER
    Archiepiscopus Milwauchiensis
    July 14, 1958

Library of Congress Catalog Card Number: 58–13624

© 1958 THE BRUCE PUBLISHING COMPANY

MADE IN THE UNITED STATES OF AMERICA

53366

ACKNOWLEDGMENTS

A book is a work of many hands and minds and hearts. Even in a work as small as this, there have been too many contributions of labor, encouragement, and generosity for specific mention of each.

A special word of gratitude, however, should be included to Rev. Stephen E. Donlon, S.J., and Rev. John A. Hardon, S.J., from whose classes in fundamental theology much of this book's contents was derived; to Rev. Vincent J. Forde, S.J., for his patient reading and valuable suggestions, and to Rev. Mr. Carl J. Armbruster, S.J., for his invaluable assistance with the galley and page proofs; finally to Sister St. Herman Joseph, C.N.D., for help in the typing of the manuscript.

JOHN POWELL, S.J.

The Feast of the Sacred Heart
of Jesus, June 13, 1958

v

CONTENTS

TO THE READER

Since A.D. 30, all real thinking and intelligent living have forced upon man a fundamental decision. Since that time no thinker in the civilized, Christian world has considered the origin and destiny of life and been able to advance an intelligent theory, nor has any salesman, mechanic, or housewife settled upon a sound plan of life without somehow reckoning with the claims of Jesus of Galilee. The demands which this Jesus has always pressed upon the human mind and heart are not soft and moldable to the contours of human comfort. Like the man, Christ, they are not to be compromised. Partial acceptance of Christ is rejection of Christ. It is His own solemn determination:

"He who is not with Me is against Me."

Every man whose life has been touched by Christianity and the claims of Christ, whatever his situation or station in life, has enjoyed the freedom of choice; but just as surely as he makes the journey over the road of life, he must sooner or later come to that fork which calls for acceptance or rejection of Christ. There is no middle path. Two billion, three hundred and seventy-eight million human beings are now in the course of that journey. Each, if he is aware of Christ's claims, has a decision to make. The importance of that decision is not minimized by the great numbers of men deciding. This is of paramount and eternal importance for every man; upon his decision will hinge everything. You and I, the boy selling papers, the telephone operator, the bus driver, the old man who hobbles down the street, and the boy next door practicing his music — we all must either take Christ in or we must rule Him out.

1

The little book you are holding in your hands is a humble treatment of a magnificent theme: the divinity of Christ and the divine authority of His Church, proved especially from the miracles of the Gospels and Catholic Christianity. These are transcendent realities which demand profound consideration both by the man who has accepted to live by them and by the man who stands before these truths in humble inquiry and quest of certainty. The one who is living by these truths needs to be strengthened in his faith which will tend to grow weak unless bolstered up by such meditation as is here proposed. He who hesitates in the presence of these truths needs this reflection, too, in order to prepare himself for the grace of faith and the acceptance of Christ's Church. A STRANGER AT YOUR DOOR is addressed to both these men, in the hope that it will help them to a happier and holier life, in and through Christ.

The pages to follow, you will find, cannot hope to impose a decision nor compel assent. Assent is exclusively yours to give or refuse. But if anyone shall find in these pages a stimulant to consider what will be the most important decision of his life, their purpose will have been achieved.

One important suggestion. Do not read these pages. Study them, think them, think around and beyond them. Turn whatever thoughts you find over and over in prayerful consideration. Let them mellow and ferment in the vats of your human mind and will. Such meditation will reward you richly. The latent energies of such a prayerful reading will reach long and wide and powerfully into your life. It will be the most important decision you have ever come to; a decision for eternity.

It is not a simple matter to struggle through the barbs and branches of thought that one must encounter in considering the claims and cause of Christ. It is so much easier to cuddle up to sleep in the depths of the forests of procrastination. But one does not find the clearing, the green slopes and flower-starred hills by shrinking from the enterprise of the trek. Nor will the sun ever break through the ceiling of such a world, and spill her warmth, joy, and light.

Chapter 1

THE TIMELESS QUESTION

Long years ago, the Jewish world could not make up its mind about a new prophet and wonder-worker. He was "the carpenter's son," this Jesus of Galilee, and yet His words were more sublime and His deeds more mighty than any recorded in the annals of man. His was a challenge that could not be taken lightly, and the question which He pressed upon the mind and heart of a man was a searching question:

"Who do you say that I am?"

The question is timeless. It is directed to all men, with no reservations for time or place. It is directed to you and to me. We cannot ignore the question, no more than we can ignore the severe condition which Christ places on salvation: "No one," He said, "comes to the Father except through me."

Who do you say that I am?

An eternal destiny hangs in the balance while each man ponders the answer he will give.

There is a boy in Korea, with death in his hands.

Across a moat of trenches there is another young boy, whose mind has grown foggy on the raw liquor of Communism.

At a bar in San Francisco, there sits a familiar patron, arguing in fuzzy tones and threadbare platitudes.

In a shack of plain boards, at the foot of the Cumberlands, a little old lady sits with needle and thread.

In Washington, D. C., there is a man with many knotty problems waiting for his decision.

A young pilot is spanning the wide Atlantic. His ears hear a melody in the steady drone of four powerful engines.

In Paris, a young composer is laboring over a delicate fugue.

There is the bright hope of a pioneer in the heart of a youthful emigrant in Israel.

Behind the Iron Curtain, there is a Communist leader with a heart for conquest and hands for destruction.

A little schooner glides and bobs on Tokyo bay; and a young Nipponese adventurer feels free and daring.

> These people are very important to Christ; just as you and I are very important to Him. However their preoccupations might seem to obscure the fact, Christ's grace is at work in these hearts, just as in your heart and mine. He presses His question.

But there is a question. An old question.

It hangs on the crisp Korean air, it penetrates the stale air of the barroom, lurks at the foot of the Cumberlands, and whines over the motors of the transport.

It repeats itself behind the Iron Curtain, in the heart of Israel, steals through the door of the Parisian apartment, and floats over the waves of Tokyo Bay.

There is a stranger at the door.

He stands patiently and always at the door of the Korean barracks, at the door of the Pentagon, outside the little Cumberland cottage.

He stands at every door which encloses human souls.

He is patient for opportunity. Days and weeks . . . months and years gather a meaningless dust.

Sooner or later, the soul will listen, and He will pose His question.

*   *   *

There will be no variation. He will put the question as simply and forcefully as once in Caesarea Philippi.
Who do you say that I am?

> All really great men have wrestled with the problem of human destiny. Only sound convictions about the destiny of man can produce the heart in a man to love life dearly yet be glad to die. No man of today possesses sound convictions, however, until he has answered the question of Christ.

It can be ignored, this question.
But ignoring can be more destructive than the havoc of a flood, more catastrophic than the atomic fission set off over Hiroshima and at Bikini.
Still there are many answers; error is possible.
But the heart that utters error in answer may be sealed into eternal doom.
Such error kills. Blinds. Creates a thousand thorns of torture. It leaves the human soul in a horrible void, without nourishment. And where there is no nourishment, atrophy and decay.
It is a foolish thing to look up quickly at this stranger. A snap judgment can be a lethal judgment. Error is too costly.
A man can override his mistakes. Almost always, if he has the heart to begin again. A public figure can regain the public's confidence which poor judgment robbed from him. An actress can charm the audience she has lost by a lifeless sequence of lines.

But when human judgment has rejected the stranger at the door of the human heart, there is no other way. The road to his destination is blocked off; a man travels at his own great risk.

Human destiny is a weighty problem.

No matter what you personally think about human destiny, you must honor history by this admission, by acknowledging this terrible importance.

You must honor Socrates and Aristotle and Plato. You must honor all the minds of profound insight which have sought to unravel this problem.

These men have written their beliefs in stone and on papyrus. They have left their hopes on canvas and reams of paper. But never more eloquently than in human blood, coursing from hearts in love with an ideal.

Reminiscences:

There was Socrates calmly swallowing the hemlock. Thousands of brave souls pouring out their lives in the gory Roman arenas. Ignatius of Antioch longing to become the food of the lions. The little "Maid of Orleans" burned at the stake.

Men are not martyrs for whims and fancies.

Heroes are not born on the fluff of featherbeds. They are born on crosses, in fires, by swords.

Nor is there a solitary soul which has sounded with the ring of greatness that was without a deep belief, a deep belief in human destiny, right or wrong.

*   *   *

The stranger is still at the door.

His lips forever form the timeless question.

But the heart of the hearer sighs. The boy goes back to his guns. The drinker goes back to his drink, and the diplomat to his decisions. The pilot checks his readings, and the little old lady is still absorbed in her stitches.

Human destiny hangs precariously on the unanswered question of the stranger at the door.

These human destinies are deferred for the moment.

He has hardly been noticed.

The origin of the question. Jesus puts the question to His apostles. Peter's answer.

Once, sitting around a fire — a solitary ball of light — in the darkness of Caesarea Philippi in Galilee, the stranger at the door sat with a group of disciples. Genesareth lapped softly in the distance.

Motley souls. Their bodies reeked with the odor of fish. The flames of the fire were playing distortions upon their weather-beaten, intense faces.

Then it was, two thousand years into the past — before the age of transports and the Pentagon, before communications and television screens — the question was born!

"Now Jesus, having come into the district of Caesarea Philippi, began to ask His disciples, saying: 'Who do men say the Son of Man is?' "

The faces of the men huddled around the warmth of the fire were masked with doubt. They looked from one to another, waiting for the first to make an answer.

Finally, one of the bronzed faces leaned forward: "Some say John the Baptist; and others, Elias; and others, Jeremias or one of the prophets."

There was a pause.

Even these simple fishermen knew what was to follow, and each prepared his answer.

One studied his rough hands, calloused heavily from mending fishing nets. Another found sudden concern in the crackle and glow of the fire.

"But who do you say that I am?" came the inevitable question.

The fisherman who had been studying his hands raised
his head slowly. His answer was deliberate. How many
times he had turned the question over in his mind.

He said simply: "You are the Christ, the Son of the living
God."

There was nothing to be added, no qualification. There had
been no note of conjecture in his voice.

Those rough hands had truth in their firm grasp.

The waters of the distant Genesareth lapped quietly against
the sandy shores.

(So many chains of reasoning about human destiny have
been forged upon the anvil of the human heart with
the tireless blows of the human mind. So many of our
best minds have looked sadly upon their reasonings,
finding them incomplete. These were razor-sharp minds
and theirs were herculean efforts; but for all their facility
with the scales and balances of logic, there was no cornerstone. There was no Christ.)

O simple fisherman, how could you know?

How could you know that the link of truth which great
minds have grasped for was solidly locked in your callous-
crusted hands?

"You are the Christ, the Son of the Living God!"

> Down through the arch of the centuries
> Christ continues to press men for an an-
> swer to His question. But not all men have
> the insight of Peter, and the rejection that
> culminated in Calvary is daily repeated
> because men will not consider Christ's
> claims.

The drama did not end with the last flicker of that fire
which lit up the faces of Christ and His Apostles.

The curtain has not fallen yet.

It has not fallen in Caesarea Philippi. It has not fallen in
Korea, nor in Washington, Paris, or Israel.

As long as new human life is given and formed in the
wombs of women, as long as there are human hearts and
human souls, the curtain shall not fall.

The acts and scenes are in endless change.

But the climax is not yet.

There is still a "little one."

And "it is not the will of your Father in heaven that a
single one of these little ones should perish" . . . in Korea,
in San Francisco, in Washington, Paris, or Moscow.

It is obvious that the world will always have a stranger at
its door.

And a timeless, ageless question, forever waiting to be
answered:

Who do you say that I am?

*   *   *

When Peter confessed so simply and so directly (and so
beautifully) that Christ was the Son of God, the heart
of Christ was warm with happiness.

But the saddest line had yet to be written.

It would be so different from the note of recognition in
Caesarea Philippi.

He would come and He would go, and one who loved Him
with a virginal love would write the story of His failure:
"He came unto His own, and His own received Him not."

To so many millions He has come for rejection.

He has come holding in His hands the "power to become
the sons of God." (". . . but to those who received Him,
He gave them the power to become the sons of God.")

The tragedy here is unmistakable. Worse than sightless eyes.
Worse than the stories of human agony and grief buried
under the wrecks of fire and flood. More hideous than

the litters, which follow in the wake of war, and the
smashed humanity which they support.

"In Him was life . . .
And the life was the light of the world . . .
And the light shineth in the darkness of the world . . .
And the darkness did not comprehend it."
"He was in the world,
And the world was made by Him,
And the world knew Him not."

*   *   *

Dear lad in Korea, look up from your guns, leveled at your
enemy.
Young drunken hope of Communism, put out your brush
fires; lay aside your irrelevant dreams of murder and
conquest.
Man at the bar, give your mind and heart a chance.
Dear lady, look up from your sewing.
Mr. Diplomat, there is a far more important decision to
be made by you.
Look up, Paris, Israel, Russia, Tokyo.
Listen again, pilot . . . boy on the bay.
There is a stranger at your door.
There is the all-important question to be answered.
Human destiny rides tremulously upon that answer of
yours.
Eternal destiny.

Destiny beyond the dirt and rains of Korea,
Beyond the bar of hard oak; far more warming than
your shot of rye.
A dream of fire to pale the spark of Communism.
A destiny to be lived, after the Cumberlands have
been worn away.
A goal beyond paltry diplomatic conundrums.
A vision to outlast Israel and the Iron Curtain.

More beautiful than the sun flashing on your silver
wings.

Deeper and wider, more vast and lovely than the
waters of Tokyo Bay and the great, restless Pacific.

Dear reader of these lines, look up!

There is a stranger at your door.

In Him is life.

The life that can be the light of your world.

The Way, the Truth, and the Life.

There is a question to be answered. Look up.

Chapter 2

THE STRANGER'S CLAIM

To answer the timeless question intelligently, an intuition of the heart is not enough. Before we place our trust in anyone, we wisely demand certain credentials, and we ask definite information. Consequently, the question is logical here: What were Christ's credentials? What was His mission? Was mankind, in any sense, expecting Christ's coming? For the answer to these questions, we must go back to the creation of the world, and to the great sin of Adam. Adam had been the delight of God at the moment of his creation. He was not destined to live forever in the garden of Eden; rather he was to undergo a temporary probation which would finally admit him to the most blessed vision of God, to the eternal bliss of heaven. By his sin of disobedience, however, God's plan was marred. Adam had willfully cast away the friendship of his maker and the gates of heaven were closed to Adam and his children. But the mercy of God comes to man in the hopeful message of the prophets. Christ's coming and His atonement for the sin of Adam and the sins of men is the great good news or gospel of the Old Testament.

Anyone who seeks admission to a man's home must have credentials; the same is

true in an even more important way of
the man who seeks admission to our hearts,
who demands our love.

A housewife is at her Saturday cleaning.

All the dust and dirt brought into her house by three mis-
chievous tykes must be fought to an unconditional
surrender.

But all the dust and dirt she is fighting is not safely gathered into the dustpan. Smudges of it are on her face.
The bandana, with which she has tied up her hair, bears
marks of battle, too.

There is only one word: she is a mess.

Now, housewives know very well when they look a mess:
someone always comes to pay a visit.

This occasion is no exception. Someone has just sounded
an alarm at the front door bell.

It is a signal for quick action: the bandana flutters to the
floor . . . the apron goes behind the kitchen door on a
well-concealed hook . . . anxious hands fluff out the hair,
and run quickly over the face (and make the smudges
into streaks).

It is now or never, and so she goes to the door with an
unbelievable air; one would never guess that she had been
ruffled . . .

Especially the man who is standing at the door, whom she
has not seen before.

How could one be expected to see through her poise and
pretended calm, as she says:
"Good afternoon."

But she is not thinking, "Good afternoon."

She is thinking, "Who are you? Why are you here? Why
are you here especially at this time when I am so busy?"

"Oh yes, of course. We have been expecting you. The
gentleman at the company said he would have a man

call. The television set has been out of order for several days. It's right in here. Will you please follow me?"

Without hesitation or doubt she leads him through her topsy-turvy sanctuary.

He was expected; he came as promised; he identified himself properly.

All is well.

Soon the television set will be working well, too.

All is routine. But if that man at the door had not been expected, if he had not been able to identify himself, he could not have taken a step into that house.

The stranger at the door . . . Is He expected? Can He identify Himself? Why has He come? Why is He waiting there?

> To understand the coming and the mission of Christ, we must turn back the pages of history until we are alone in that solemn silence when only God existed.

Digression is the only choice.

The book of human history is a large, heavy book.

So large and so heavy is this book that it has never found the life long enough or the author daring enough for its research and writing.

Historians are excused from knowing the whole book. Any one chapter which has been mastered wins the diploma of approval.

With a sigh of unreal regret, we take this great, imaginary book into our hands. We place it on the floor and from a standing position begin to turn its pages.

We will start from the back . . . where the ink is not yet dry, and the sentence not yet finished. These last pages are more familiar anyway.

The last pages are of paper, but others are of cloth, pressed leaves and reeds, bronze, and finally tablets of stone.

We begin the backward journey to seek the beginnings of human history.

The pages are lifted with effort and carefully.

As we proceed into the arduous task, the names, places, and events grow less and less familiar. Soon it is unfamiliar soil over which we walk. The milestones are progressively confusing.

There is doubt at this point: Can one finish?

Then, just before the end — really it is the beginning — there waits a reward.

A familiar name: Adam.

Adam. The father of all men. The father of work and pain, suffering and death. The father of thirst and hunger, the father of a thousand miseries. Father of hospitals, of every cry that has pierced the night that his father's sin brought to earth. Father of insanity. Father of cemeteries and courts of law. Father of all the evil riot in our bodies. Father of the darkness and chaos in our souls.

But, for all that, our father.

We must not hate. We cannot disown.

      *   *   *

With a silent satisfaction the front cover is turned.

The book is once more closed.

We now stand alone. Stand before the first word of history could be written . . . before the world we have known . . . before the mountains and the valleys . . . before the first gigantic wave of the Atlantic rammed against a shoal . . . before the first bird gave music to the world . . . before the first howl of passion from the depths of the jungle . . . before the first footprint of man . . . before Orion and the Milky Way . . . before the endless, depthless blue and the blazing sun.

We are alone.

But we are not alone.

". . . Before the world was made, I am!"

In the whirl and toss and roll of imagination we can wipe away all else. But He is! God is.

The infinite, eternal, almighty God.

What was it like?

Was He lonely without the world at His feet? A foolish thing to think about an infinite God. Infinite in His joy, His ecstasy of love. Happy beyond the most daring sweep of imagination.

We have passed the limit, the foremost limit, of the book.

We cannot go beyond the author.

We can never go beyond the pen that did the writing, the prime originality from which all things have come: the infinite love of Him, who before the length and breadth and depth of all creation

is . . .

We stand with God at the sacred moment when He brought into being all things that have being: the creation of the world.

This was the love, the power, the wisdom that, in the beginning, spilled and overflowed.

"In the beginning God created heaven and earth.

And the earth was void and empty, and darkness was upon the face of the deep.

And the spirit of God moved over the waters.

And God said: 'Be there light!'

And light was made.

And God saw the light that it was good; and He divided the light from the darkness.

And He called the light Day, and the darkness Night.

And there was evening and morning one day.

And God said: Let there be a firmament made amidst the waters and let it divide the waters from the waters.

And God called the dry land Earth; and the gathering together of the waters he called Seas.

And God saw that it was good.

And He said: Let us make man to our image and likeness; and let him have dominion over the fishes of the sea, and the fowls of the air, and the beasts, and the whole earth.

And God saw all the things that He had made, and they were very good."

All in the flash and thunder of an almighty will!

Be there waters. Blue and pure waters. Large, rolling bodies of restlessness. The ripple and skip of streams. The placid lakes over which the trinket of His moon may lay a strip of yellow ribbon, when day is done and the sun has set.

Be there earth. Deep, rich soil. Long rolls of fertility. Majestic snow-capped mountains to stand like kings over His plains and meadows. Carpets of restful green. Clusters of flower and vine.

(Be enchanting, earth. Be a legacy and a message: tell the life placed in your support how beautiful is He, who "before the world was created . . . is.")

Be there man. The crown of creation. The image and likeness of his author. Made to love and be loved. Sharer in the life of God Himself. Led by an irresistible instinct. Formed by Love to return love.

*   *   *

It is good for man to go back, to stand thoughtfully at the place of his origin.

It is good for man to go back and kneel silently at the feet of his God.

The story of creation and man, the lord
of creation, is marked by an almost immediate catastrophe: the terrible sin of our
first parents, Adam and Eve.

Our hands are back at the heavy pages of history. We have
looked with eyes of amazement upon the almost unbelievable act which we call creation.

Where before there was nothing, absolute nothing, there
is now a vast and wonderful universe; flowers, hillsides,
brute beasts, and . . . two human beings.

Our hands are back at the pages of history, back through
the story's beginning, back through the story of Adam
and Eve.

Back over that terrible line: ". . . you have eaten of the
tree whereof I commanded you that you should not eat!"

Here, for the first time, is the sword of sin thrust into the
side of God.

But it was human blood that flowed from the wound in
answer.

Every child that is brought forth upon God's earth shall
bear the scar of that wound, and wear the badge of his
father's rebellion.

But there is a deeper grief.

The doors of this world swing wide.

But the doors of heaven are sealed beyond the power of
man to open.

The doors of home are closed. Heaven is barred; man has
lost his home.

The beauty that once charmed the very eye of God — the
beauty of His own reflection — is an orphaned beauty;
parentless and homeless by man's own cleavage, beyond
human repair.

This is the deeper grief: man cannot go home.
(Think of it. Think of this sorrow: to be barred from
home!)
The familiar sounds are never to be heard again. The longed-
for sights will not be seen. The voice, desired by the
deepest roots of instinct, forever silent.
There is no warmth, no solace. Man is an alien to his father
and home.
The night is cold.
And the lonely heart of man cannot plead for justice. Jus-
tice has been done: beyond the plans of man to undo.
(Our hands still turn pages. . . .)

> The prophets of the Old Testament were
> men whom God inspired to interpret the
> mind and will of God for their fellow men.
> Through the voice of the prophets God
> gave the world hope again, gave the heart
> of man a great expectancy that mercy and
> forgiveness would be brought to the world.
> God would send the Messias.

The heart without hope wanders blindly down the dark
streets of human history.
Then . . . a light flickers briefly in the distance.
Hope is reborn. Hope courses through the once-frozen veins
of the corpse of mankind:
One, who is born of woman, shall open the door which
shall lead us from our exile.
One, who is born of woman, shall open the door of home.
"I will put enmities between thee and the woman, and
thy seed and *her* seed; she shall crush thy head."
This God says to the serpent of doom.
And the voice of our great God resounds against the breast

of the patriarch, Abraham: "I will make thee a great
nation . . . and *in thee* shall all nations (all the kindred
of the earth) be blessed."

. . . The kindred of the earth shall be blessed. Blessed with
the mercy of a father, our Father.

But how? How can mercy surmount the high wall of
eternal justice?

Jacob lays new and live coals on the fire of hope: "Juda,
thee shall thy brethren praise. . . . The scepter shall not
be taken away from Juda, nor a ruler from his thigh, *till
He comes that is to be sent, and He shall be the expectation of nations.*"

God will not leave us orphans.

"A star shall rise out of Jacob and a sceptre shall spring
up from Israel!"

The voice of the Psalmist raises the prophetic message to
a new pitch of hope: " 'Thou art My son, this day have
I begotten Thee. . . . I will give Thee the nations for Thy
inheritance.' "

"He shall protect the lowly among the people, he shall save
the children of the poor, and shall crush the oppressor."

God will send mercy to His people.

> Not riding on the condescension of written decree.
> Not through the sound of human voices.
> God shall Himself inhabit our land of darkness and
> tears.
> A child He shall come.

"A child is born to us, and a son is given to us, and the
government is upon his shoulders; and his name shall
be called Wonderful, Counsellor, God the Mighty, the
Father of the world to come, the Prince of Peace!"

He will come clothed in our human inheritance. He will
feel the weight of our woes.

He will conquer by blood . . . His own blood:

"I was as a meek lamb, that is carried to be a victim."

Here is the resurrection of hope.

Here is hope at its brightest.

Here in the prophetic visions, uttered by tongues that have felt the purifying sting of live coals.

The voice of the prophet splits the midnight sky of despair. Hope sends a wedge of light screaming earthward . . . into the heavy hearts of men.

God shall send the Son that He has begotten!

The gaping birthmark of Adam's sons will be cleansed from the foreheads of men. The wound shall be closed.

The gulf, the infinite gulf, that separated man from his true home shall be spanned by a new bridge of mercy.

Even if tears of gratitude coursed down the furrowed cheeks of mankind, it would be understandable.

There is warmth and joy in the very thought: Once more, man can go home!

The hope-bearing voice of the prophet: Look to your horizons, Juda.

One day, with the setting of the sun, a star shall arise out of thy bosom, O Jacob.

He will come "that is to be sent"!

"Protector of the lowly . . . the expectation of the nations . . . the inheritance of the nations . . . the Son whom God has begotten . . . Salvation of the children of the poor . . . Crusher of the oppressor . . . Wonderful . . . Counsellor . . . God the mighty . . . Father of the world to come . . . Prince of Peace!"

"A child shall be born to thee!"

Born in the helpless form of a child.

Born to die. Born for victimhood. Born to be the lamb led to slaughter.

Rejoice, fallen heart of man, for in the death of that lamb you may find life!

The prophecies find their fulfillment in the
most solemn moment this world has ever
known: the Incarnation of the Eternal
Word of God. The Son of God becomes
a man.

This was the prophecy. This was refurbished hope, confirmation that there would be a stranger at the doors of
the world. A thousand years before He would appear. A
thousand years of hope. A thousand years of counting,
marking time. Like counting beads, knowing that you
will reach the end and the gem fastened there.

A thousand years of hope . . . a thousand pages later in the
history of man — our hands fly through the pages — the
words of confirmation. The prophecies are fulfilled.

(Long into the past, a thousand miles back on the highways of history, like a sound of rising from the loneliest
grave, the quivering voice of the hoary prophet had said:

"Behold the Virgin shall be with Child.

And she shall bring forth a Son!")

The confirmation so long in coming, strikes like thunder
at the heart which pounds wildly in the breast of
humankind.

Ah! There it is. There it is beyond denying:

The angel has spoken to a little maiden in Galilee.

"Behold you will conceive in your womb, and shall
bring forth a Son, and you shall call His name . . .
Jesus!"

*   *   *

This was the moment. An angel and a maiden. And a
human race and human hope hanging on the words of
the maiden.

Quietly she spells out the hope of man:
    "Behold the handmaid of the Lord.
    Be it done unto me according to thy word!"

                    *   *   *

And in that instant:
    "The Word was made flesh."

                    A colloquy addressed to Mary, the Im-
                    maculate Mother of God, whose thoughts
                    are searched as she holds her newly-born
                    Child close to her heart, in the manger at
                    Bethlehem.

All this, even this, thousands of years after the first painful
    surge of hope and expectation had awakened the hearts
    of Adam's children.
    ". . . She brought forth her first-born Son, and wrapped
    Him in swaddling clothes, and laid Him in a
    manger . . ."

                    *   *   *

Young Mother, as you looked upon those tiny hands,
did you see them extended to all ages to come? Did you
see them at work with hammer and nails in the carpenter
shop? Did you see them raised, beautiful with power and
majesty, to still the squall over Genesareth? Did you see
them holding the bread that was to become His Body,
the cup and covenant of His Blood? Did you see those
tiny hands brimming, running over with forgiveness for
His "little ones"? Did you see those tiny hands and
feet covered with blood on Mt. Calvary? Did you see
them reaching out to the last man that will ever live on
this earth?

As you wrapped those tiny feet. . . . Did you know how
tirelessly they would pursue the hearts of men over the
dusty roads of Galilee and the world? Did you know
they would walk the pavements of Houston, Chicago,
and Paris, the cobbled roads of Amsterdam, Rome, and
ancient Bruges? Did you know that they would board all
the ships in the harbors of men? Did you see them tramp-
ing the boulevards and back streets of the world, pressing
through jungle paths, along every human-made way? Did
you see them standing at every mansion and gas-lit
tenement? Did you see them at the doorstep of man?
Hands filled with mercy. Feet made to follow. Wherever
there is a "little one," there He will be. This, thy Son,
young mother, a stranger at every door, behind which
there is a human soul and a human heart, and human
sickness and human grief. Did you know that it was for
this that He had come?

The stranger at your door comes uniquely
announced through the voices of the prophets. No other figure of history has come
heralded in this way; nor is it possible
except by the intervention of God, who
thus sends His eternal Son into the world
that we might recognize Him and claim
Him as our Messias and Saviour.

Dear housewife, at your Saturday cleaning, the stranger
standing at your door has come uniquely announced.
He has been expected with an expectation as old as the
garden of Eden.

The Expectation of the Nations, He has come to you, to
claim the rightful debt of your heart.

We may search our minds . . . we may search the long
and large book of human history, but we shall find none

other that comes as He has come. Ask the names and
places we learned in school:

Julius Caesar, who were your prophets?

Gustavus Adolphus, how could we have expected you?

Where was the notice of your coming, Bonaparte?

Were you the expectation of your people, Disraeli?

Bismarck, did you carry any credentials other than
your insatiable lust for "steel and blood"?

Were the people of France ever told to look to you,
little island of Corsica?

What was the truth about you, Arpinum? Did you
know that Cicero would immortalize your name?

If you think too long about these questions, they will dis-
turb you.

The realization will startle you: you will have to face it
even if you don't like or want it.

The truth of it will not be obscured. Sometimes the eyes
can hide their tears, but the mind of man is fashioned
for a greater honesty.

Here was a life "written" before it was lived!

Here was a man whose biographers might have been his
most ancient forebears. Here was a narration before the
narrative.

You could say "fantastic anachronism" except that it would
be too fantastic.

We are here face to face with the Almighty, in whose hand
alone the answer lies. The mouth of the prophet
opened, but the voice was the voice of God.

David, Isaias, Jeremias, Daniel,

Michaeas, Zacharias, Malachias:

How else could you know?

How else could your dim eyes have focused on the
little town of Bethlehem in Judea?

How else could you have listed an as yet unbegotten
genealogy — an unlived descent?

How could you know:
Born of a virgin?
Announced by the "voice of one crying in the wilderness"?
How could you see Him entering Jerusalem? How could you know the power in His hands? How could the silhouette of a cross not yet erected cast its shadow back over to the centuries to be seen by your eyes?

Yet these are the facts.

This is the gist: a life was written, by the prophetic inspiration of God, before that life was lived!

Housewife, mechanic, salesman, student: take down the family heirloom (the Bible) which stands in the bookcase. Take down David, Isaias, Jeremias; take down Daniel, Michaeas, and Zacharias. Read thoughtfully for yourself. These are very old words you will read, gray with the grayness of three thousand years. But their meaning is as fresh as the current moment.

Read and think, and . . .

Go to the door! Go to the expectation of the nations, the meek lamb of God, the star risen out of little Nazareth.

Yes, the expectation of all the nations of the world really and truly is waiting at your door . . . a stranger at your door.

This is the One of whom God said, through the prophet Isaias:

"Behold My servant. I will uphold Him.
My elect: My soul delights in Him.
I have given My spirit upon Him.
He shall bring forth judgment to the Gentiles.
. . . He shall be no respecter of persons.
He shall bring forth judgment unto truth.
. . . And the islands shall wait for His law.

. . . I have given Thee for a covenant of the people,
For a light of the Gentiles.
That Thou mightest open the eyes of the blind,
And bring forth the prisoner out of the prison,
And them that sit in darkness out of the dungeon."

It is important to you that the "elect of God" should stand
at your doorstep. It means so much more than your set
of ceramics, in which you take such well-deserved pride,
more than your guns, polished and ready for the season
to open; more than your drinks and discussions; more
than your bridge and your season pass to the opera.

It is far more necessary for you to know this and do something about it than to enjoy twenty per cent from that
last sale, which you so cleverly put across, and that week
end in Florida, which is tickling your imagination.

> The instincts which have forever driven
> great thinkers to seek an answer and solu-
> tion to the great problems of human life
> and which drive every one of us who wants
> to find some meaning in our day-to-day
> lives can be satisfied only by One: the
> Alpha and Omega, the beginning and the
> end, the Messias, the Christ.

Thoughtful men have dipped deep beneath the shiny sur-
face waters of life to find that truth which alone can
satisfy the hungry human heart, and so many have sadly
come up with sand in their thirsty mouths: with Buddha,
Brahma, Atman, Varuna; with Zeus, Mazda, and the
god of the sun.

Do not laugh at them. While others were making gods of
sex and stomach, and (in spite of what Copernicus
would discover) making themselves the center of the
universe, these men were in search.

In search of a cornerstone which had not been laid.

Our generation uncovers the same instincts in man, but in a different way:

> Our generation parades ceremoniously and unabashed to lie on the couch of the psychiatrist.

But the urge and instinct in them and in us is one and the same.

We are looking for a meaning, for a reality: we do not know what it is or where we may find it, but that thirst and pain drive us to the four corners of the earth to find that which has all the time been waiting at our door.

This decision at our doorstep; this concern at our threshold.

> This Messias . . . this Christ.

The thrill of discovery awaits the opening of that door. The thrill of recognition. The thrill of a man named Andrew, who once raced breathlessly over a road in Bethany beyond the Jordan, to tell his brother the news — the news which is at your door — "We have found the Messias!"

The meaning for Andrew and Peter, the meaning for you and me, is one and the same!

> The same hope.
> The same salvation.
> The Hebrew tongue called Him their "Messias."
> The Greek-speaking peoples their "Christ."

There is one great thing in your life:

> He belongs to no one more than to you!

> The story that follows is the story related in the Gospel of St. John about the meeting of Jesus and the Samaritan woman at the well of Jacob. Although she is slow to understand, the patient Jesus at last succeeds in telling her that He is the expected Messias.

It is in the gospel narrative of St. John that we read the incident to follow.

One bright and hot day, Jesus was passing through a little town, called Sichar, in the district of Samaria in Palestine. The journey on foot from Judea had been long and tiring, and the remainder of the journey to Galilee was not a happy prospect for the blistered and burning feet of the little group that traveled with the Master.

So they found their way to an ancient landmark in Sichar, called very simply, "The Well of Jacob." It was a deep, refreshing shaft of water for which the villagers gave thanks to their father, Jacob. The hallowed tradition, which became known far and wide, was that the grand old patriarch had bequeathed this well to his son, Joseph, and to all the thirsty flock of natives that would come there to draw water for the following day.

It had become a "town square" long before the days of town squares, where many a bronze-skinned peasant first made the acquaintance of his neighbor. These simple folks had no super markets, office buildings, or bridge clubs. These familiar institutions would be the social arsenal of a different and distant age.

Here it was, then, by the side of this sunken cylinder of gray stone, that He sat for a moment of rest.

The virtuous disciples had hurried off to the town proper to buy some food.

Jesus was alone in the hot sun, awaiting the visitor appointed by Divine Providence from all eternity.

Jauntily over the parched road, carrying a water jar on her head, she came. A Samaritan woman. She was a stranger to Him, just as He would be to her.

A complete extrovert, this woman born out of time.

Had she dwelt among our skyscraping giants of steel and stone, she would have raised many an eyebrow in the circles of polite society.

As she approached, she stole a quick glance at the stranger
  sitting by the side of the well.

Her ever urgent impulse to conversation vaporized in that
  glance.

No one could mistake Him: He was a Jew!

And even Jews who are lost would not stoop to ask a
  Samaritan for directions, let alone exchange a pleasant
  "hello."

And she, being a Samaritan and proud of it, bore a disdain
  similar to the disdain she had projected into His mind.

So she grasped the rope at Jacob's well with routine facility,
  and while she was fastening the end of the rope to her
  pail, a soft surprise came from the side of the well:
    "Would you please give Me a drink?"

Her eyes widened in surprise, and she fixed them suddenly
  on this man. Perhaps she had been a bit hasty in her
  judgment. Perhaps this man was not really a Jew.

The second survey confirmed the first.

She cleared her throat and said:
    "How is it that you, although you are a Jew, ask me
      for a drink . . . me, a Samaritan woman?"

For all the pointedness in her question, she was hardly
  ready for this:
    "If you only knew the gift of God, and who it is that
      is saying to you 'Give me to drink,' you perhaps
      would have asked of Him, and He would have given
      you *living* water."
    (Could He expect her to know that "in Him was
      life"?
    Could she be put to wonder?)
    Her answer immediately deflated all hopes for any
      wonder or understanding:
"Sir, this well is deep, and you have nothing to draw with.
  So where could you get this living water?"

Her mind was sadly fastened to the thought of the water
that can be ladled into a jar.

"Are you greater than our father Jacob who gave us
the well, and drunk from it himself, and his sons,
and his flocks?"

His answer was directly to the point:

"Everyone who drinks of this water will thirst again.
He, however, who drinks of the water that I will
give shall never thirst; but the water that I will give
him will become in him a fountain of water, spring-
ing up unto life everlasting."

He is holding out to her the life of the spirit, a life of devotion and worship. He is holding out to her the quite
indescribable gift which we call a participation in the
life of God. It is the only water that will quench the
thirst of a human soul.

But her mind does not see what it is that He offers. She
still thinks in terms of water as in Jacob's well. She
foolishly imagines that He is going to give her a supply
of that water which will save her the hot wearisome trip
to "Jacob's Well."

"Sir, give me this water that I may not thirst, or come here
to draw."

You or I would have given her up as hopeless.

You or I would have impatiently regretted bringing the subject up, and we might have dismissed the subject with
a casual, "It's been hot today, hasn't it?"

But you and I do not wait at doors that will never open,
either.

He sees one alternative.

He will make her see the power that could have caused
a hundred wells to come gushing from the arid deserts
of Samaria.

"Go call your husband, and come here."

"I have no husband."

"You have said well, 'I have no husband,' for you have
had five husbands, and he whom you have now is not
your husband. In this you have spoken truly."

Then, there was dawn in that mind, bright and clear.

"Sir, I see you are a prophet. Our Fathers worshipped on
this mountain, but you say that at Jerusalem is the place
where one ought to worship."

He explains softly and simply that salvation will come to
the world from among the Jews.

(Never would this woman stand so close to her salvation.
Somewhere her soul is still living. It must be that if she
is among the blessed in heaven, her salvation grew out
of this day, this hour, these words that He spoke to her.)

"God is spirit, and they who worship Him must worship
in spirit and truth."

He struggles to make her see that living is not completely
external. Neither is worship completely external. Such
people, as this simple Samaritan woman, can talk in
terms of water, because it slakes the thirst; water weighs,
cools, washes, and extinguishes fire. The senses can argue
to this. But there is more to worshiping and loving God
than the argument of the senses. There is the heart
which only God sees. We must kneel. We must utter
prayers. We must worship gathered together, in a body
(God promised to bless that prayer where two or three
are gathered together in His name); — but all these
things must be a reflection of that which God alone can
see: the heart.

But she is sadly poor at subtleties:

"I know that the Messias is coming (who is called
Christ), and when He comes He will tell us all
things."

She has demolished any hope of indirection or suggestion.
And so He says it simply and directly:

"I who speak with you am He!"

> In a sense which is very real we are all
> typified by the Samaritan woman who met
> Jesus at Jacob's Well. Like her we are all
> seekers. Like her, we may pray, we shall
> find Jesus and all search shall be ended
> for us.

St. John tells us that the poor woman went off in such a
hurry to tell the others in the little village that she left
her water jar behind her.

We might wonder why St. John bothered to record this
fact. We might wonder if there isn't in this small thing
a grand significance.

Each of us has a water jar . . . an empty water jar.

We wander through life, wanting to find and to fill our jar.

The water that this man seeks is money. His neighbor
seeks the cooling draughts of fame and honor. His brother
has eyes only for the flow of hilarity that round after
round of sex, liquor, and song deceitfully promise.

And each is met by a stranger at the well of his desires.

And each is promised:

> Who drinks of the water that I will give shall never
> thirst! The water that I shall give shall become in
> you a fountain of water, springing up into life
> everlasting.

But law shackles life . . . and so, in the driving pains of
our thirst, we sometimes make gods of sex, of our money,
or of one or other well-coddled passion. We sometimes
make one of these our Messias.

And the wellsprings at which we drink poison our souls.

But there is just enough Samaritan thickness in us to
miss the point completely . . . to forget (as we all forget at times):

"The water that I will give shall become in you a
    fountain of water, springing up into life everlasting."
We forget the stranger that waits so patiently at our door.
Some day, we must pray, the bright and clear dawn will
    break, and we will happily leave our water jars at the
    wells of this world, and race breathlessly to announce to
    all that will hear:
    I have found the Messias . . . I have found the Christ!

> This is what makes the acceptance or rejec-
> tion of Jesus a thing of awesome impor-
> tance to a man: he may be dealing with
> God. In fact, only God would press the
> demands upon a man that Jesus did not
> hesitate to impose. Still, the honest and
> teachable man has every right to ask
> Christ to prove His claims. It is, in fact,
> the part of intelligent faith, which is the
> faith that God honors in the Christian
> believer.

But these are the days of overstated advertisements.
Our grandmothers talked about a "grain of salt."
We are the "salt-barrel" generation, then.
If housewives bought all the gadgets which "will literally
    cut your housework in half," there would soon be no
    drudgery for the queen of the castle.
If our new cars were the ones advertised, repair shops would
    soon be closed for want of repairs.
This "salt-barrel" generation is well schooled.
The simple fact with us is: Prove it!
Wrongly or rightly, we feel that the knocks and bumps of
    twenty centuries have made of us a progeny of skeptics,
    but in fact three-dimension is not new. We are not
    the first to say: "I have to see it with my own eyes."

The eyes of ancient Jerusalem wore three-dimension glasses, and the minds we sometimes slough off as "outmoded" thought of length and breadth and depth, long before our modern physicist found them one day in his laboratory.

Such were the eyes . . . such were the minds that first reckoned with the acceptance or rejection of Jesus of Galilee.

He could profess to the woman of Samaria that He was her Messias. . . . He could pronounce that Apostle (Peter) *blessed* who proclaimed Him to be ". . . the Christ, the Son of the Living God."

He could say to the pressing demand of the Jews that He say whether or not He was the Messias, the Christ: "I tell you and you do not believe!"

He could console the grief-stricken sister of the dead Lazarus with His claim: "I am the resurrection and the life; he who believes in Me, even if he die, shall live; and who-ever lives and believes in Me, shall never die!" (. . . words which only God can rightly say!)

In the face of an agonizing death, He could tell the Jewish Sanhedrin, in whose hands His fate rested, that He was the Christ, the Son of God; and He could boldly add that someday each of them would stand before His judgment.

He could lift up the sagging hearts of His disciples on the road to Emmaus by His explanation of how "the Christ" (Himself) had to suffer these things before entering into His glory. . . .

But, before we can be expected to leave our precious water jars, to go in search of "living waters". . .

He must prove it!

We do not say this with the cunning of a professional skeptic.

There is no cynicism, disguised or outright, in this demand.

No more than the child, whose wide eyes are gradually

opening to the world of persons and things . . . whose innocence we may have lost, but whose honest curiosity we share.

We want to be saved from the dishonest pretense, and stripped of that sophistication which humans sometimes wear like a new dress or a suit of clothes. We would be washed of all malice.

But, we would still ask: Why? Why must I accept the Christ?

This is indeed no simple matter. This is not a matter of days or weeks; or months or years.

This is not as ephemeral as last Saturday night's canasta game, the score of which escapes us at the moment (it was close, anyway).

The demands of Christ — the demands which Christ writes into the contract with His believer — are not as forgettable as the grocery bill last Christmas.

This is a question of eternity . . . a measureless, endless existence, where the stakes are high, success unbelievable and failure irreparable and eternal!

This is a question of an eternal joy that "eye hath not seen nor ear heard . . ."

This is a question of everlasting fire.

Christ's demands are not for Sunday or Monday, for this week or that . . . there is no time clause in the contract.

Christ comes saying that He teaches and confers life. . . . He speaks of the Kingdom of Heaven as His very own . . . the Kingdom of God is His right. . . . He insists without compromise that whoever shall believe His teaching (and in Him) shall be saved . . . who will not believe will be damned into everlasting, unquenchable fire. . . . He says that His every word is the word of God because He is the Son of God. . . . He is God:

"I and the Father are one!"

Oh no, my soul, this is not a simple matter.

Let us review the claims that Christ made
to men. It would be a foolish thing to
make any judgment of Christ without first
considering carefully that which He said
about Himself. We cannot say that Christ
was merely a very holy man if He said He
was God. There is no middle ground here:
either Christ was what He claimed to be
and therefore worthy of all our love or
He was an impostor and worthy only of
the pity and compassion we give to
deceivers.

Christ claimed to be the Messias.

"I who speak with you am He," He told the Samaritan woman. Now, to the Messias, in Hebrew tradition, belonged the honor and worship of all men.
The very name, Christ, is the Greek equivalent of
the Hebrew, Messias. Consequently, each time that
He used this name (Christ) or accepted its usage,
He affirmed that He was the Messias.

Christ claimed to be a teacher, sent from God to teach a
divine religion.

"You say that I am a teacher . . . and so I am." Thirty-
three times in the gospel narratives He accepts this
title. The religion that He teaches is the central
theme of all His teaching about the Kingdom of
God and the Kingdom of Heaven. The one purpose
of His teaching was that men might be saved by
believing in this teaching. ". . . preach the gospel to
every creature. He who believes and is baptized shall
be saved." The religion directly revealed to men by
Christ was that of God our Father: "My doctrine
is not mine, but His who sent Me."

Christ claimed that His religion must be embraced by all
men (to be saved).

"Go, into the whole world and preach the gospel to
every creature. He who believes and is baptized shall
be saved, but he who does not believe shall be
condemned."

Christ claimed to be the natural Son of God (and therefore
to be of the divine nature of God). When the apostle,
Peter, proclaimed Him to be "The Christ, the Son of the
Living God," Christ solemnly declared that Peter was
"blessed . . . because flesh and blood have not revealed
this to thee, but My Father who is in Heaven." Again:
"He who does not honor the Son, does not honor the
Father who sent Him." His natural sonship must not be
mistaken; He is the Son of God, and He is therefore
God: "I and the Father are one." To the same point:
"Do you not believe that I am in the Father and the
Father in Me?" This is the substantial unity of the Divine
Persons in God from all eternity: "And now do Thou,
Father, glorify me with Thyself, with the glory that I had
with Thee before the world existed."

*   *   *

The urgency of the matter. I must make
my decision about Christ carefully and
promptly. This is far too important a matter to wait.

These, then, are the claims to be proved.

One may comfortably dismiss the claims of the door-to-
door salesman. A man can wait to find out if the latest
style of automobile or washing machine or can opener
will stand the test of time.

One can pass up "the bargain of the century" and still live
with himself somehow; still think of himself as a fairly
reasonable man.

One can gamble when the stakes are printed on paper.

But, when the stakes are everlasting, when mistakes can be eternally disastrous, when man may be dealing with his God, when there is an unqualified and all-important *must* to be considered . . .

A sound mind will put away the slide rule which determines the laws of chance. This is no gamble; there is no fall of dice, no cut of the cards to prove a man right or wrong.

Gambling here (on the contents of a water jar as against the claims of Christ) makes less of an appeal to reason than curling up before the fireplace to play "Russian Roulette."

Chance plays no part when one is dealing with God.

With such a basic sanity man must put to the test the claims of Jesus of Galilee.

There is no deferring the all-important decision, when next year may be too late, next month or even next week may find the brief summary of your life — a name and two dates — written on a stone over a rising mound of earth . . . your grave.

In dealing with God, nothing is left to chance.

So, with a purpose and a determination as fixed as the mountains, I must consider these claims and demands of Christ.

I must decide whether or not I am dealing with God.

"Whoever shall believe in Me . . . the same shall be saved!"

"Whoever does not believe in Me . . . the same shall be condemned!"

Oh no, my soul, this is not a simple matter.

Chapter 3

THE BLIND SEE AND THE DEAF HEAR

The case for Christ's divinity, the substantiation of His own profession that He is God, could well be rested with the persuasion of the prophecies which heralded His coming. Such prophecies are obviously and totally beyond human resource, and so thoroughly genuine in their religious implications that they must be taken as the divine corroboration and approval of the words and the works of Christ. But over and above such a persuasion, Christ Himself leaves no doubt. Over and over again He repeats His profession that He is the Son of God, that He has the same divine nature as His Father:

"All things which the Father
has are Mine."

And over and over again this profession is confirmed by miraculous power. A true miracle, one which is beyond suspicion, is an extraordinary intervention of God into the affairs of this world. It is a mark of God's approval, when the miracle is implored as a standard and motive for credence, since it is entirely reasonable to presume that God would not thus intervene to establish error or falsehood. It is entirely reasonable to presume that God's power would not be in the hands of one whose mouth uttered lies. The life of Jesus is a pattern of the power of God. Omnipotence flashed from His finger tips and resided in His softly spoken words. But, for all the many proofs that Christ gave of His divinity, the culmination of His own proof lies in the astounding and unique miracle of His life: His resurrection from the dead.

The miracles of Jesus have two sides. They reveal the tender compassion that He felt for the sick and the suffering, and the great power that faith has with God. Not a less significant side is the probative aspect of miracles. When the imprisoned John the Baptist sent his disciples to find out if the man everyone was talking about was the Christ, Jesus gave those disciples one credential: The blind see, the lame walk, the lepers are cleansed, the deaf hear, the dead rise, the poor have the gospel preached to them.

St. Matthew tells us in his gospel narrative how the man who came to announce Jesus of Galilee, one John the Baptist, was imprisoned by an arrogant power, called Herod Antipas, for stirring up the muddy waters of this ruler's conscience, for daring to suggest that there was in the world a power greater than the power of Rome, which he wielded in a limited sort of way.

Herod was a law unto himself.

It is fateful to suggest to such a man that he cannot lawfully steal his brother's wife. This was the "suggestion" of the bold Baptist.

No doubt (Herod thought) after this crazed hermit had cooled his heels in a dank dungeon, his enthusiasm for righteousness would settle like the dust after an April rain.

Of course, it would be otherwise. The lustful tetrarch would eventually discover that the fire in this man would not be so easily extinguished. But there were shows in the arena to be watched; spicy, tart wines to be sipped; hundreds of slaves to be whipped; and so, not much thought could be wasted on this bearded fanatic, now safely behind the indestructible walls of an Herodian prison.

The kindly rays of the sun were well shut out of that cell which John occupied, but rumors find their ways around corners, through iron gratings, and even through the barricades of prisons.

And so, one day, the word seeped through: there was a man about who was doing very unusual things, and His words were more unusual; He spoke and it was difficult to challenge His authority. He said He was the Christ, the Son of God.

There was exhilaration in John's aching bones at the very thought, and he whispered a question into a friendly ear.

It was the same question you or I would have asked.

It was the same question we are asking ourselves at this very moment.

"Are you He who is to come or shall we look for another?"

*   *   *

And so, while Jesus was moving from town to town, always at His work of preaching, He was confronted one day, by the messengers of John, and John's question was put to Him.

Now this question was not as innocuous as we might think at first. . . . Not just thirteen words which could be answered once and for all in a single word.

The answer would be just as significant to John as it is to you and me. A simple "yes" would not be enough. The fearless man in King Herod's prison wanted more than this. You and I are looking for more than this.

John knew the prophecies of the Old Testament very well, we can believe. He knew the vast importance of the question he had put. He knew that if this man were really the Son of God, really the Messias, the answer would be a proof, not a simple, cheaply made assertion.

Today we might put it this way: the question was loaded.

There is a theory that John himself knew it was the Christ. The proof was asked not for himself, but for his followers who would bring the question to Jesus.

Still would it be true that without confidence that this was the Christ, John could not have borne the stale and damp prison air with a singing heart any more than you or I can bear the four walls of our lives.

But if this is the Christ, then for John and for you and me it is enough!

We might, therefore, say that the answer to John's question is the answer to ours.

"And Jesus answering said to them:

Go and report to John what you have heard and seen;
The blind see, the lame walk.
The lepers are cleansed, the deaf hear.
The dead rise, the poor have the gospel preached to them!"

* * *

The significance of this answer and of the miracles of Christ is clear if we understand the meaning, nature, and proving force of miracles in themselves. If Christ claims to be God, then we may very rightly expect Him to do what only God can do. Mir-

acles, by their very nature, only God (or
someone acting in the name of God)
can do.

Here is an answer freighted with meaning.

With meaning that the disciples of John could grasp, that
you and I can grasp.

If a man boasts that he is strong, then he must be prepared
to do the things which only a strong man can do.

If a man claims that he is a genius, then he must do the
things of a genius in proof of his claim.

If a man says that he is God . . . then he must do the
things which only God can do.

But . . . what can only God do?

The answer is not easy. Be patient.

We live in a world of laws . . . laws which man has not
made, and which man cannot deny or surpass. Every
drop of water in the ocean, every grain of sand on the
beach, every autumn leaf that flutters and spins to the
ground is subject to laws.

Every body, gaseous, liquid, or solid, observes laws. The
poor scientist would certainly have to find another occu-
pation if the matter he worked with operated by a different set of laws each time he looked through his
microscope or worked with his cyclotron.

Without these laws, doctors could find no remedies, engi-
neers could build no roads, and teachers could not teach,
for there would be nothing to be learned.

We are introduced to these laws from birth.

In the baby's first wail a law is at work.

The first time a child falls or drops a spoon a new law is
beginning to come clear to him.

A little boy puts his hands into the filled sink, and water
runs over the sides onto the floor: at least one law will
be learned.

The child looks up at the stars and wonders what holds them up there . . . wonders why the sun and the moon do not come crashing down upon the earth . . . wonders whatever happened to that skinned knee he had two weeks ago.

And what he really comes to accept as the ordinary course of events is really a set of laws.

Every nature has its laws. And despite the infinite number and minute detail of these laws, there is not a single law court, because: There are no violations, no exceptions to these laws! Except . . .

Except when the blind man suddenly sees, the lame suddenly throws away his crutches, or the paralyzed man arises from his bed and walks.

Except when the hideous body of the leper is cleansed . . .

Except when the deaf hear, the dead rise. . .

. . . and the poor have the gospel preached to them!

To understand these laws in detail is impossible.

But to know their origin is not so difficult.

The laws of the first wristwatch were determined by the man who made the first wristwatch.

The principles of the first steam engine were determined by the man who made the first steam engine.

It is simple enough.

The laws of the solar system, the skies, the earth, and man himself are likewise determined by their maker.

. . . Once more, in the silence of our reasoning . . . we find ourselves at the feet of God.

God, who made all things: who made the skies and the earth, who made the forests and the meadows, who made the soul and the heart of man.

If, then, we see before our eyes a true and real and undeniable exception to these laws, we know that we have encountered a power beyond the realm of nature, a preternatural power:

An angel, a devil, or God.

But even the brightest of angels . . . the darkest of devils:
They know the power of God, the power of God's law.
They can do only what God permits them to do.

The angels, the more-than-eager servants of their creator,
are forever doing His will and His work.

But, ah! There is the Devil, forever after his own will and
his own works: forever trying to bring the darkness and
the confusion of his home upon the suburbs of humanity.

He can catch the eye, stir wonder in the mind; enter
where all is tranquil and leave with all things stormy.

The Devil can take the mind of man up to the mountain-
tops, offer to make the world at man's feet his plaything.

The only thought of the Devil is: to deceive . . . to put the
ring of many promises through the nose of the man who
is not alert and lead him around like the saddest of brute
beasts.

He cunningly sings the thrush's song, but when the careless
nature lover goes to find the source of melody, it is a
panther of lust that leaps from the branches.

This very cunning of the Devil leaves a question, does
it not?

> When the blind eyes see and deaf ears hear, and cures
> are effected . . .

There is a doubt:

> Have we felt the touch of God's hand?
> Or is it the song of the thrush?

The puzzle is not without a solution.

At least this much is certain:

> When the blind behold the world of color and shapes,
> when the blocked channels of hearing are opened
> again to the sweetest music of sound, when the
> bodies of the dead walk again . . .
>
>> because one who is holy has called upon God
>> or

called upon the powers in Himself because He
is God . . .

There is no place for mystery.

If God, who is enamored of the souls of men, could hear
the prayer of a loved one, and allow the Devil to lead
that loved one astray, into the endless mazes of error,
then:

There would be one name only for God:
Deceiver.

But God, we know, does not, God cannot deceive!

Deception is as foreign to the nature of God as truth to
the father of all lies, the Devil.

> External phenomena which seem to be of
> miraculous nature must be judged care-
> fully; must be judged by the circumstances
> that surround the phenomena: what has
> gone before, the phenomena themselves,
> and the effects they produce. A miracle is
> good and holy in its beginning, middle,
> and end.

There is an old adage: *Circumstances speak.*

Applied to the matter at hand, we might say that when
the circumstances are the fragrance of holiness and a
devout prayer to our Father in heaven, then we can be
sure:

It is the hand of God that does these things.

When the circumstances are the black billows of a sul-
phurous smoke, a selfish motive, dishonesty or pretense
in any form,

God is not there.

This the Jewish people knew twenty centuries ago.

"He casts out devils in the name of Beelzebub."

So it was tremendously significant that Jesus of Galilee

could have challenged the scorning and accusing
Pharisees:

"Which of you can accuse Me of sin?"

In the long record of human opinions, no one has ever
rightfully accused this Jesus of depravity. . . .

Men have denied His claims; accused Him of being a
gullible soul. Others have honored Him with the
insult of

"A mere but benign Socrates of Religion."

But the charge and the challenge will be forever un-
acceptable:

"Which of you can accuse me of sin?"

When the word of such a person opens eyes and ears, brings
forth men from the dead, cures the dying, and cleanses
the leper, there is only one thing for the reasonable man
to admit:

This was the power of God.

When the Baptist's disciples brought back the answer of
Christ, John knew the meaning. Eyes must be closed
to avoid the conclusion.

It is the bedrock reality upon which a man stands, when
he confesses faith in: ". . . Jesus, the Christ, God's
only Son, our Lord."

*   *   *

Words will never be as eloquent as works.

Jesus knew that.

You and I know that.

And the florist who insists that we "Say it with
flowers" also knows it.

And so the life of Jesus of Galilee is a wealth and a welter
of wonders.

The power of God flashes out time and time again.
Jesus never gave a more eloquent proof of the
Godhead in Himself.

Here was the claim to be God . . . here was the power of
God:
>At most unexpected times.
>In most unexpected places.
>Water becomes wine . . . a leper is made clean . . .
>an empty net suddenly bursts with a haul of fish . . .
>a man walks on the water . . . five loaves and two
>fish feed a multitude . . . a fig tree withers . . . and
>a man takes off the wrappings of death.

This is not a mere biography. This is a study of the power
of God!

>A digression on the power of God! An-
>other aspect of this power: trust and con-
>fidence in the God to whom this power
>belongs.

How often we forget that awesome power.
We labor and we fret. We long to fill our barns and our
water jars; each night we say "good night" to a school
of well-cultivated worries, and we know that we shall
meet them again in the morning and live with them
always.
We will be forever bothered and eaten away by these para-
sites as long as we forget:
>An almighty hand thrust into our lives.
>An almighty hand in our hand.
>An almighty source of strength at our side.
>A hand raised over our lives that was once raised
>over the turbulent waters of Genesareth and the
>leper at Capharnaum.

Things go wrong. Sickness strikes, debts pile up.
Our hearts grow weary and sick. And we forget the voice
(of God) that once told us:
>"Come to Me, all you who labor and are heavily
>burdened, and I will refresh you."

We forget that the best way to know the tender and cur-
ing touch of God is to be sick.

*   *   *

Having considered something of the nature
and purpose of the miraculous, we proceed
now to a consideration of some of the
miracles that Jesus performed. The first such
miracle which we will take up is the cure
of the paralytic at Capharnaum.

The first three of the four original biographers of Jesus tell
us of the following incident. It occurred in a small
village called Capharnaum, toward the north of Galilee,
just off Genesareth or the Sea of Galilee.

The course of His travels had brought Jesus away from His
own town, and now He was decided to return.

It was not long before word of His arrival had made the
rounds and the people of Capharnaum were gathering
together to hear Him speak.

On one such occasion, a young paralytic was carried by
four friends to the house where Jesus was speaking. These
four men were not only well trained but apparently quite
determined.

When it was clear that entrance through one of the ordinary doors was impossible because of the bulging crowds,
these four friends carried the paralyzed man up onto the
roof. There they made an opening, and lowered the
helpless figure down till it rested at the feet of Jesus.

The young man on the cot lay still and helpless, and no
doubt he was worried that this unusual entrance would
offend Jesus who had been speaking.

But the heart of Jesus was magnetized by such scenes of
suffering. Without invitation (though the young man was
obviously being brought to put His powers to the test),

He advanced slightly, bent over the cot, and looked down upon the face of this boy.

A tender sympathy was written on His striking features.

The youth looked up and saw Him standing there . . . he was used to pitying glances, looks of sympathy . . . but there was something very different . . . strangely different . . . in the spell of that countenance.

Here was power and majesty and yet extreme tenderness looking down upon him.

Words would not come.

And then Jesus said to the boy:

"Take courage, Son; thy sins are forgiven thee."

(This did something rather obvious to that crowded room.)

Eyebrows lifted; ears strained as though they had not heard correctly. Eyes widened and stared; and in the shock of such surprise a man at the far wall sent an impulsive but communicative elbow into the ribs of the one next to him.

The words seemed to hang on the now silent air:

"Thy sins are forgiven thee."

Later Jesus would commission His Apostles to the merciful work of forgiveness of sins in His name. But until that historic moment . . .

Until He would Himself declare:

"Whose sins you shall forgive are forgiven them.

Whose sins you shall retain are retained" —

Until that moment, the forgiveness of sins was the exclusive right of God alone.

This was what only God could do: "Thy sins are forgiven thee."

It did not require a penetrating mind to sense the meaning of those words.

He was standing there in the shaft of sunlight that streamed through the opened roof, and He was saying this:

He was saying that the power of God was His!
He was claiming to be God.
The shock was electric.
"And behold, some of the Scribes said within themselves,
'This man blasphemes!'"
"Who can forgive sins, but God alone?" they asked.
And the word they chose — blaspheme — was meant to say
this: Here is a mere man who says that He has the power
to forgive sins, which power belongs to God alone. This
man is saying that He is God.
And, in fact, it would have been the most terrible blas-
phemy, except for this one thing: He was God.
But the amazement that was to sweep down upon the
little room of electrified Jews had not yet reached the
peak of its full impact. It had hardly begun.
Jesus had not taken His eyes from the numb and helpless
form under His gaze.
And yet with a knowledge
        that knows whenever a sparrow falls,
        that knows the count of leaves in the summertime,
        that knows each blade of grass,
        and the hearts and thoughts of men,
            He asked:
        "Why do you harbor evil thoughts in your hearts?"
There was, of course, no reply.
It is embarrassing and silencing to have your most secret
thoughts pulled rudely from the sacred privacy of your
mind and laid naked before the eyes of all.
It was just as embarrassing then as now.
Then Jesus put another question:
        "For which is easier to say, 'Thy sins are forgiven
        thee,' or 'arise and walk'?"
There was only a vast and significant silence. Staggering
minds faced the conclusion, and anxious hearts sensed
a climax.

If the power was in this man to make this helplessly dam-
aged body arise and walk, then it had to be believed that
His was the power to say: "Thy sins are forgiven thee."
Their bodies stiffened, their muscles drew taut, and in the
silence of expectation, they instinctively leaned forward.
Everyone tried at once to shift to a vantage point to have
the fullest possible view of the scene.
Then Jesus said:

"But that you may know that the Son of Man has
power on earth to forgive sins" — (turning to the
paralytic, He said) — "Arise, take up thy pallet, and
go to thy house!"

All eyes fell and were riveted to the figure lying on the cot,
the boy whom they had all seen carried about for many
years, the boy whom they had pitied for many years . . .
". . . and he rose, and went away to his house."

*   *   *

We are told that "when the crowds saw it, they were
struck with fear, and glorified God. . . ."
So was it always with Jesus of Galilee . . . if men would
but hear Him, if men would only let Him: He would
cause them to give glory to God.
When the powers of evil are at work, the fruit of that
work is an evil fruit; men do not fall on their knees and
glorify God; they become monsters of lust and passion,
and the glory of God is not on their tongues, nor in
their hearts.

*   *   *

We do not hear again of the young man who came before
the merciful glance of Jesus in such an unusual way.
He merely "arose and went away to his house," as he
was told to.
Still, we can be sure of this:

He never forgot the power in that face which had
    looked down upon him in pity.

He never forgot the words: "Thy sins are forgiven
    thee . . . Arise, take up thy pallet, and go to thy
    house."

Nor can we.

The eyes of the Almighty had viewed that scene . . . the eyes
    that have seen all things from all eternity.

Almighty ears heard the words, the promise and the proof.

Our almighty Father saw His power in the power of His
    Son . . . one and the same power . . .

    And received the glory of men.

Had it been otherwise, God would have given the proof
    of His power to the forces of deception, would have
    branded as true what could never be true, would have
    allowed men made to His image and likeness to be lost
    to the forces of evil and destruction.

Had it been otherwise — Had Jesus not been God — God
    Himself would have been blessing blasphemy.

It could not have been other.

The voice of God had been heard unmistakably:

    "This is My well-beloved Son in whom I am well
    pleased!"

             *   *   *

          The second miracle: Jesus restores to life
          the only son of the widow of Naim: "Young
          man, I say to thee, arise!"

Naim is a small village at the southern end of Galilee,
    which nestles at the foot of Mt. Thabor.

St. Luke tells us of a time when Jesus was passing through
    this district and encountered a funeral procession.

It happened as Jesus and His disciples approached the gates
    of the town. From a distance they had heard mournful

cries of the professional wailers, a traditional part of funeral rites in those days in that place.

As the procession came into sight, Jesus and the disciples politely and silently stepped to the side of the road.

The litter of death was weighted with the body of a youth who had died with all of life before him. There was a unique sadness in the sight: the sadness of a flower that is plucked too soon.

Sadder still was the sight of the frail woman who walked behind the litter, for, as St. Luke tells us, she was a widow, and this dead boy had been her only son; had been the center of all her dreams and hopes; had been her whole life.

Death had robbed her of that life, those dreams and hopes. She knew now what a deep thing grief can be; she knew now how death could be wonderfully enviable, when there is nothing to live for. She knew how fiercely the human heart can ache.

No human heart could have witnessed that scene without experiencing a sharp stab of sympathy . . .

Much less the divine heart of Jesus of Galilee.

And so, the procession of death was unexpectedly interrupted, as a stranger from the side of the road approached the anguish-laden widow.

We are told that His first words were what you or I might have said to the lady:

". . . Do not cry."

That was all He said.

Simply: "Do not cry."

The wailing had stopped. One could not tell how long it would be before this stranger with runaway emotions would recover himself and get off the road. There was still quite a walk to the cemetery, and those carrying the boy's litter were already arm-sore.

So it was an impatient glance that the party of mourners

fixed upon Jesus, in their hurry "to get it over with."
But Jesus, turning, "went up and touched the stretcher;
and the bearers stood still. And He said, 'Young man,
I say to thee, arise!'"
A sudden realization came clear to those who stood by;
it was obvious, once you thought of it: this poor man
was insane! Of course He was! No one in his right
mind would dare to stalk boldly through such a proces-
sion, interrupting the last wails of regret that would be
sounded through the streets of Naim for this boy.
But it was not perfectly clear that the man was demented,
until this: until he walked over to the lifeless and cold
form and said:
"I say to thee, arise!"
These were the things they thought. And then . . .
Then, "He who was dead, sat up, and began to speak. . . ."
The imagination delights in picturing the scene that must
have followed.
St. Luke says only this:
"And He gave him to his mother."
As to the impatient members of the procession, it was the
same result as before:
"But fear seized upon all, and they began to glorify
God, saying . . . God has visited His people!"
"God has visited His people." How well you reasoned, little
band of mourners in ancient Naim.
Dear widow of Naim:
Did you ever forget the comforting hand that sup-
ported you in the throes of your grief? If you had
lived a thousand years could you ever have forgotten
the depth and strength and consoling power in the
words: "Do not cry"? Did you ever dream back to
the wonderful moment? Did you see that face? Did
you bless that hand which gave your only son back
to you?

Did you hear that voice in the roar of the surf and sweep of the winds? It was there. Did you see that hand in the starlit sky? In the height of the hills and the delicate veins of a leaf turning gold? It was there. Did you feel the power and strength of that man in every subsequent moment of your life? Dear widow, it was there.

Twice had He given you that much loved son. For His was the power that once caused life in your womb . . . And His was the power that gave that life back to your embrace, back to your aching heart, just outside the gates of Naim.

The same power then.

The same power now . . . and always:

The power of God.

Some personal reflections on the miracles of Christ: the meaning and importance of these miracles to me. The power and tenderness of God in my life.

Such scenes leave the heart impressed and even glowing.

But what is more important: they weight the mind with a conviction. A man claims to be sent from God. Claims to be God. And the power of God thunders in His words. Streams from His hands.

Even the saltiest of a "salt-barrel" generation must say in his heart, as a Roman centurion had said centuries before, when he opened the side of Christ with a lance:

"This was indeed the Son of God."

*　　　*　　　*

Supposing a man does believe . . .

Supposing a man does believe that once there lived on the earth a man called Jesus of Galilee . . . He said He was

sent from God to be a teacher of men . . . He said He
was God. And He proved His claim beyond all shadow
of doubt. He did the things which only God can do.
Might I ask: so what?

So what is Jacob's well today? What do Capharnaum
and Naim mean to me:

Me, a banker on Wall Street?

Me, an underpaid and underappreciated grocery
clerk, a real first-class flunkie?

Me, the latest rage of Stage and Screen?

Me, the most popular girl on the campus?

Me, the wretched little nobody with five hungry
kids and a drunken husband?

Me, the old man who has had his hour on the
stage, and is ready for oblivion?

Me, a sweaty and grimy factory hand whose ironic
contribution to civilization is driving nails?

What does Jacob's Well, Capharnaum, Naim mean to me?

What does it mean to me, today, that God visited His
earth and His people in the distant and shadowy past?

What good is that now to the poor "sucker" who hasn't
got a shirt to cover his back, or food to fill his stomach?

Pretty thoughts about God's tenderness won't heat a tenement house, filled with starving children and crawling
rats.

It won't help the desperately hungry and the homeless
to know of Naim. And the stuffy, overweighted rich won't
be thrilled to the marrow to hear that the Messias once
put in an appearance at Jacob's Well in Samaria.

So what, you ask, as millions have asked before you: So
what?

So this perhaps:

The Messias was not only in Capharnaum and Naim and at
Jacob's Well. His power was not only for the unsightly
leper, the blind, and the paralyzed.

His words were meant to be the food and the text of life not only for the Jewish people twenty forgotten centuries ago.

He hasn't run out of mercy or "living water" after three years of public life or three thousand years. Whatever is His is limitless.

The rewards He promised and the pains He threatened were not just for then, but for always.

The little ones whom He would guard and pursue with a tender and fatherly love were not enclosed within the fence of one nation or one age.

The Messias is waiting at your door, even where there is no knob . . . even if you have no house.

The power that once streamed from His almighty hands, the power of Naim and Capharnaum is yours, if only you will put your hand into His.

The teaching of Christ is not outmoded like grandmother's book of table manners. It is for your life. Yes, your life, here and now.

His teaching is for all men, everywhere, in all times.

Believe this, if you can: You are Christ's "little ones," the "little one" that Christ loves so tenderly. Believe in Him and trust in His love for you.

Now follow this carefully:

This is what Capharnaum and Naim and Jacob's Well mean to you.

If Christ's claims were true . . .

If He is God . . .

Then His is an infinite knowledge . . . He knew and He knows all things.

In His divine mind all things are known in one, eternal now.

At once He sees the sparrow that fell yesterday, the lily that will blossom tomorrow.

If you accept these things . . . there is no way around it

... this was the fact:

At Jacob's Well, at Naim, on the Sea of Galilee, in
Capharnaum, and on Mount Calvary ...

He was thinking of you.

He was thinking of you in your dingy office, in your sweaty
factory, in the deep, dark coal mine where you disem-
bowel the earth of her riches, in your mansion, in your
tenement. Wherever you work, wherever you live, wherever you are.

He was thinking of your sorrows. He was thinking of you
in the gnawing pains of your loneliness ... in the bot-
tomless sensitivities of your human heart.

But the most beautiful thing is this: He loves you. From all
eternity He has loved you, wanted you, wanted to possess
and be possessed by you. He has wanted to be wanted
by you.

You may not believe this ... now.

But someday you shall realize very clearly.

This you can believe right now (perhaps it is the easiest
thing for you to believe). Someday you will die. The
thin veil that separates this life from eternity will
be snatched away, as though it were a thin silk scarf.

Then you shall see: with such a terrible clarity.

Will this realization then come as a painful one? Will you
be torn apart with grief that you missed the point for
such a long time?

Consolation waits for you, now, at your doorstep.

Go to the door of your life, and let Christ in.

Go to Him because you need Him. Go to Him
because you want to return His love. Go and rest
in the power of Capharnaum and Naim.

Perhaps we do not know what Christ means today because
the door of our lives is closed tightly ... or because we
are blithely unaware that He is waiting to enter our lives
and mean everything to us.

The third miracle: Jesus raises Lazarus from
the dead. "I am the resurrection and the
life. He who believes in Me, even if he
die, shall live. And whoever lives and believes in Me, shall never die."

Let us go back again.

This time to an incident in the life of Jesus, related by St.
John. (Jesus knew that someday you would read or hear
of this incident. If nowhere else, then here in these
lines . . . in this book. It is true that as God, in His
divine mind He knew all things. Even in Bethany, over
nineteen centuries ago, back in a drafty little cottage by
the brook of Cedron where this incident takes its setting
[Do not be surprised] . . . you were there. You were
there in the eye and focus of His thought. You were there
in the vast and warm love of His heart. In His every
action and word, He was thinking of you.)

Bethany was a little village in northern Judea, not many
miles from Jerusalem, at the side of the brook of Cedron.

In little Bethany, there lay dying a man named Lazarus.

As death hovered on silent wings over this man, his griev-
ing sisters, Mary and Martha, sent an urgent message
of their need to Jesus, whom they had known and loved.
(Maybe sometime in the past you, too, have sent such
a message . . . to a doctor or a mother or father to come
quickly to a dying loved one, perhaps. Then you will
be able to understand the anxiety in the hearts of these
women. You will know what it is to need someone . . .
badly.)

You know perhaps how your heart would have reacted to
the message which Jesus returned to Mary and Martha.
It was hardly to be expected.

They had written: "Lord, behold, he whom Thou lovest
is sick!"

And He had said simply:
    "This sickness is not unto death, but for the glory
    of God, that through it the Son of God may be
    glorified."
You or I would have twisted and scraped the words for
    meaning, for some possible, consoling meaning.
We would have read it again and again:
    "This sickness is not unto death. . . ."

            *   *   *

St. John tells us that for two days afterward Jesus stayed
    in the region of the Jordan.
Why did He wait?
And then when the two days passed — although there had
    been no message of any kind — He who knew all things,
    knew:
    Lazarus had died!
We might wonder what was the grief of Mary and Martha.
    He to whom they had learned to turn in every grief,
    whose power they had seen so clearly to be the power
    of God, who had calmed the winds and the waves; —
    He had promised that this sickness would not bring
    death. But now, one thing was certain: Lazarus was dead.
We might wonder if it wasn't nearly a double death. How
    easily the love and faith of the sisters might have died
    with their good brother, in the darkness of that night
    of trial.
"Then afterwards He said to His disciples, 'Let us go again
    into Judea.' "
The disciples protested. The Jews had attempted to stone
    Him in Judea. He could not return now. It would be
    His death.
But His eye was not on Himself. His eye was on "His little
    one."
"Lazarus, our friend, sleeps," He said.

"Sleeps?" That was a puzzling thought. The reaction of the
disciples is convincingly normal; with the simplicity of
a child, they answered:
  "If he sleeps, he will be safe."
"So then Jesus said to them plainly,
  'Lazarus is dead.' "
There was a sudden and reverent hush; an "Oh!" that only
the inmost heart hears and feels.
Then Jesus added ". . . and I rejoice on your account that
I was not there that you may believe. But let us go to
him." (Let us not forget that we too are with Jesus, in His
thought. Let us not forget that He rejoiced on our account
also: that we might believe.)
Then the disciple, Thomas, who had learned well and be-
lieved deeply in the blessedness after death of which Jesus
had spoken, began to think earnestly about:
  That reward which "eye hath not seen, nor ear
    heard . . ."
Now Thomas was convinced that a return to Judea would
not only mean death for Christ, but also for those who
walked at His side.
By this time, his reflections had swept Thomas up to a
gratifying loyalty and heroism:
  "Let us go also that we may die with Him."
If Jesus was to die, Thomas would perish with Him. A
single eye and a faithful heart.
And so the little band departed for Bethany.
Jesus knew all the while that someday they, too, would
rejoice that He had not been there when Lazarus had
died. For in some distant day those disciples would suffer terribly for Him, and they would need the strength
that the experience soon to be theirs would afford.
Word that He was coming had meanwhile passed before
Him over the road that leads to Bethany, and so the ever
faithful Martha went out to meet Jesus.

As He went along, He saw her approach, His divine eyes
looked into her heart. He saw there an indestructible
faith . . . faith of steel. He knew that her words would be:
"Lord, if Thou hadst been here my brother would not have
died."
He saw the hope that still burned brightly in her heart and
on her quivering lips:
"But even now I know that whatever You shall ask of
God, God will give it to Thee."
And Jesus answered: "Thy brother shall rise."
But Martha misunderstood His meaning:
"I know that he will rise at the resurrection, on the
last day."
Then Jesus looked sympathetically into those eyes reddened
with weeping, and glistening now with fresh tears . . .
into that face disarrayed by grief but radiant with faith,
and He whispered softly: "I am the resurrection and the
life; he who believes in Me, even if he die, shall live;
and whoever lives and believes in Me, shall never die.
Do you believe this?"
Her answer was perfect. It must have been a warmth to
the heart of Jesus:
"Yes, Lord, I believe that You are the Christ, the Son
of God, who has come into this world."
This is the faith that moves mountains . . . the faith that
brings the dead back to life again.
"I am the resurrection and the life. He who believes in
Me, even if he die, shall live; and whoever lives and
believes in Me, shall never die!"
How many aching heads and hearts would lean upon
the soft comfort in those words . . . In dimly lit
rooms where an angel of death is awaited in silence
. . . In the hearts of many a mother and father told
of the death of their son on some distant battlefield,
or buried under the billows of the ocean tide . . .

By the side of a cemetery plot where a dear one lies
at rest . . . In the painfully great voids of life left by
the visitation of death:
  Places never to be filled again.
  Voices no longer heard.
  The disappearance of a comforting hand and a
  consoling smile.

In all these, one consolation: "I am the resurrection and
the life!"
For these words to Martha were a new comfort.
  Death was proclaimed a door . . . a beginning . . . a
  birth . . . a springtime.
The unbearable sting is gone forever.
The world will still seem to wobble and fall when death
comes to steal a piece of the human heart.
War Department telegrams will never cease to wring the
hearts in mothers and fathers with terrible grief . . .
Human hearts will continue to ache and ache . . . But:
  The grief and the sorrow and the ache will not be the
  grief and the sorrow and the ache of despair.
There is a comfort now . . . a new consolation . . . a new
hope:
  "I am the resurrection and the life!"
It is the hope in the heart of every boy going into battle.
The hope of the world riding on sinking ships and in falling
planes.
The hope that the heart holds out when the doctor places
all in God's hands.
The hope that will someday be yours and mine in our last
moments.
The hope of every man who will believe in Him.
  "I am the resurrection and the life. He who believes
  in Me, even if he die, shall live!"

              *   *   *

After His arrival, Mary and Martha took Jesus to the tomb of Lazarus, who was four days dead.

Then, we read three words we must never forget:

"And Jesus wept."

What was the meaning of these tears?

Did they stand for the weakness of man? Uncontrollable floods of emotion which break over all men at times? Did the heart of Christ give way under the weight of grief?

Wherever we reach for an explanation of these tears, our hands always seem to return empty.

There seems to be only one answer:

Jesus wept that you might know,
that Mary and Martha might know,
that I might know:

An infinite sympathy . . . a heart that would always have tears for human grief . . . An infinite understanding of human sorrow and the human heart.

The love of Christ will always and everywhere bend over the wounds of humanity: the torn flesh and the torn hearts.

The tears that fell from the eyes of Jesus, and coursed down His cheeks in an unexpected show of emotion are a reminder of that love and sympathy and understanding which God will always have for men.

Too often, we forget those tears. We exile ourselves from that belief and comfort which alone can assuage our grief and loneliness: the belief that someone is there in the darkness of sorrow . . . the comfort in knowing that He wishes only to console.

It seems quite certain that a man will never feel abandoned in grief, or alone in his sorrow, if he will just remember three words:

"And Jesus wept."

Without some realization of the compassion of God for

us, the world becomes a world of thorns and brambles,
because there is always a time when the words of sympathy that others offer are distant, unfeeling, uncom-
forting. And there are times when the words of others
are not offered.

There should never be a time when we will not be able to
find comfort and strength in the eyes of Jesus, filled with
tears; in the vision of God's head bowed in sorrow.

Lazarus was dead.

*   *   *

Lazarus had been laid in a cave, and a stone stood guard
at the entrance.

And so it was that Jesus said:

"Take away the stone."

We can easily imagine the concern and regret that swept
up into the face of Martha, as she said:

"Lord, by this time he is already decayed, for he is
dead four days."

The answer of Christ gave the first bright hint that the
power of God would break forth once more, and the
grief in Bethany be banished:

"Have I not told you," He said quietly, "that if you
believe you shall see the glory of God."

"They therefore removed the stone."

"And Jesus, raising his eyes, said, 'Father, I give Thee thanks
that you have heard Me; but because of the people who
stand round, I spoke, that they may believe that You
have sent Me.'"

The lowering clouds of doubt are about to be parted by
power and the light of God is about to stream down
upon men.

Always and everywhere Christ asks men for the complete
gift of their hearts. He asks men to suffer for Him. He
asks a service of sacrifice.

He demands of every man a love greater than that which a man has for his very mother and father. He asks of some a trust and a faith till the last drop of blood has been poured out. He asks men to endure crosses and fires and the fangs of lions for His sake . . . to be ground into the dust for Him.

And so He wanted to prove His right to make these demands. He knew much better than we that it is hard to bleed, hard to endure, hard to die. Men would have proof that to bleed, endure, and die for Him is a glorious thing and not a sad delusion.

So He would offer a proof that men could never deny. A proof that death for His sake means life and glory and reward, and satiety for the thousand thirsts of the heart.

For, knowing all things, He knew: Men do not die for words.

Consequently, "When He had said this, He cried out with a loud voice: 'Lazarus, come forth!' "

The die was cast.

For the little group that stood at the mouth of that cave, in which Lazarus had rested for four days, decision about Jesus of Galilee was at a crisis.

If He is God, then all doubt will be carried away by the evening winds in Bethany, and human eyes shall see what is humanly impossible. But if life does not stir in that little cave of death, all His claims and all the demands which He asks of men must be erased from human memory. The book will be closed once and for all. Jesus of Galilee will be just one more in the long line of impostors about which history books tell.

"And at once he who had been dead came forth, bound feet and hands with wrappings, and his face was tied up with a cloth."

*   *   *

This was to be one of the last legacies of Jesus, for St.
John tells us that when the news came to the ears of
the already anxious Pharisees, it set off a fuse of panic
and frenzy.

"If we let Him alone as He is, all will believe in Him,
and the Romans will come and take away both our
place and our nation."

So it was. The picture of the angry face of Rome sent chills
through these poor, bloodless men, and they weakly determined that it was expedient to barter truth for Roman
complacency. The supreme reward: the smile of Rome.
What would it profit a man to gain the whole world,
but suffer the loss of the smile of Rome?

Had these poor men, the Pharisees, but known. Had they
been able to look forward, as you and I can look back,
and see the once-great colossus of the Roman Empire,
see it a sleeping giant whose angry power has long since
been forgotten, lying in the dust of time, harmlessly
dead, mere brittle bones for the excavator and historian.

Had they been able to see the growth and harvest of that
seed planted in Naim and Capharnaum and Bethany;
the devotion that would creep like a wild vine over the
face of the earth, watered by the blood of a million martyrs, nurtured from the wounds of persecution, ever growing, spreading and reaching to the four corners of the
earth, over the hills and valleys of nineteen centuries . . .

Had their eyes been able to see this, the line that follows
in St. John would certainly have been left unwritten:

"So from that day forth their plan was to put Him
to death!"

But just as the Pharisees would lament, "Behold, the entire
world has gone after Him!" and eventually put Jesus to
death on the cross of disgrace, so Lazarus, too, according
to their plans, would pay with the life that had been
restored to him.

It is not surprising.

A living, walking proof of the power of Jesus was a danger-
ous thing.

It would be a betraying tolerance and an insult to the glorious empire of Rome to allow such a man to walk the
streets as he pleased, all the while reminding the people
that there was in the world a power much greater than
Rome.

This man, Lazarus, was lighting too many fires of enthusiasm, and these were not healthy for the men upon
whom Rome had laid the fearsome hand of her trust.

This Lazarus was a reminder. A proof in flesh and bones.
His very presence was like a message in the sky:
"I am the resurrection and the life!"

It was not to be tolerated.

                    *   *   *

The whole doctrine of Jesus, His claims, His demands
walked about in the person of this living confirmation.
They walked about in the market place and in the temple.
The people who had all paid their last respects to Lazarus
were now paying another kind of respect to Him who
had called Lazarus from the dead. In fact, they were
quite carried away and wanted to hear all they could
of this Jesus of Galilee.

For the Pharisees this was dreadful. The alarm had been
sounded. This was a challenge that could be met only
by death.

And so, one day, according to a tradition, Lazarus appeared
no more.

                    *   *   *

But Lazarus was not unique. If the days of miracles are not
over, neither are the days of Lazaruses. Would it be an
overstatement to say that the world is filled with Lazaruses? Fires . . . that will not go out.

Today Lazaruses are burning brightly behind and beneath
the Iron Curtain. Burning in distant and uncivilized
lands. Burning in our big cities and our sprawling farm
lands. Burning in factories, in offices and food marts.
Burning on the highways of this twentieth century.

These witnesses and proofs of the power of God!

These people are veins of life running through the body of
humanity, which is sick with a thousand ills.

Men and women and little children whose souls are alive
with the love and faith of Mary and Martha, alive with
love and enthusiasm for Christ.

Somewhere in the life of each of us there is a Lazarus, a
reminder that God is all-powerful, all-merciful.

Wherever there is a life lived for Jesus alone, there is a
Lazarus. A living proof of God's goodness and power,
walking the streets of our lives, pregnant with hope, and
radiantly confident with the confidence of one promise:
"I am the resurrection and the life!"

Are we not, in another sense, all of us Lazarus . . . we
have all received life from the same almighty will that
determined to cry, "Lazarus, come forth!"

Just as a charred ruin stirs images of the flames, and the
dawn looks back into the darkness, so each spark of life
in every man:
    the propulsion of infinitely numerous thoughts
    and desires from his mind and will . . .
    the recoil of joy at a morning in spring . . .
    the innocent ecstasy in the face of a happy child . . .
    and even the pain in a man's heart;
recall the flame of God.

For life in each man is a Lazarus.
    A reminder of the voice once heard in Bethany:
    "I am the resurrection and the life. He who believes
    in Me, even if he die, shall live; and whoever lives and
    believes in Me, shall never die."

And we, too, must rejoice that He was not there . . .
    . . . that Lazarus had actually died . . .
    That we, too, might believe.

> The culmination of Christ's proof that He
> is God, and the final miracle of our con-
> sideration: Jesus raises Himself from the
> dead.
> "After three days I will rise."

Love is more a thing of deeds than words.

And love in deeds has never reached a higher climax than
on a day almost two thousand years ago on a rising hill
in Judea called Calvary, the place of crucifixion.

Greater endurance for love has never been written in human blood . . . Here meekness and courage met in one
flesh. Strength and tenderness, in magnificent propor-
tions, joined in one man beyond any hope of repetition . . .
    . . . in the crucifixion of Jesus of Galilee.

That day has been solemnly laid into the neglected vaults
of time, trampled into oblivion by two thousand years of
ever changing feet, by two million distracting concerns.
The vision has lost its focus. The image is dull.

But if a man should believe with a consuming belief, if he
should believe deeply and devoutly and with his whole
heart, so deeply that he almost kneels again on Mt.
Calvary and sees the bloodcovered body of Christ, if
a man should once look up into the dying eyes of Jesus
of Galilee:

He will never forget. The heart will not be in him to dare
whisper, even when no other man can hear, "Jesus, You
ask too much of me." He will never kneel in the shadow
of that cross, and demur:
    "Jesus, I have now suffered enough for You."

Nor would a man think of saying: "I'm sorry I do not

have the time or inclination to consider Your cause and demands."

Nor would such a man ever doubt the mercy that God has for man. If he could only believe:

"Father, forgive them, for they know not what they do!"

Men can find no refutation for this kind of mercy. Men do not refute the forgiveness that comes from bleeding lips . . . lips quivering with pain . . . the pale lips of death.

At three o'clock that afternoon, the voice of Jesus, once laden beyond belief with power, was heard to gasp:

"It is finished!"

His head dropped down upon His chest.

Jesus of Galilee was dead.

Humanly speaking, it was the end. It was the final period mark, humanly speaking. The great *finis* to a great life had been written with hammer and nails. A wellspring of mercy and power had been drained to the last drop . . . humanly speaking.

The Jewish high-priests and the Pharisees could glory now in the triumph of the moment.

And the breezes which had carried word of Jesus over the churning waters of the Mediterranean into the very precincts of Rome were cleared now of suspicion and rumor. Even in Rome, this man had caused a catch of the breath, but now breathing was regular and easy . . . humanly speaking.

As the darkness of the night settled that evening over Judea, there was obviously a note of finality. Even in the heavy hearts of the little band of mourners that mourned the blood still wet on the rocks of Calvary.

Mourning was mingled with fear in the hearts of the disciples, as they huddled together behind the barred doors of the little cenacle. If the Jews decided to rip out of Judean soil every root and fiber of enthusiasm planted by Jesus, their blood would also redden the soil.

That was to these scared disciples a terrifying thought.

So, there was a sense of triumph and a sense of defeat that
night in Judea, for:

Jesus of Galilee was dead.

. . . humanly speaking.

But He had never said that the venture of His life was a
human venture. In fact, His insistence had been otherwise. The laws which all men must obey were thin and
brittle bands, which broke apart at His word, and at
His touch.

In the transcendence of His Godly powers, He had made
it very clear that He was outside and above human
calculation.

Of Him there could be no "humanly speaking."

For one thing, when a man is dead — humanly speaking —
he is dead. There is no return.

But Christ had promised that, after the hammers and nails
had done their work, He would of His own power walk
back through the walls which bar return, and be once
more in their midst. Three days He would remain in
the land of the dead, by His own prophecy and promise.

"For even as Jonas was in the belly of the whale three
days and three nights, so will the Son of Man be
three days and three nights in the heart of the earth."

But, after those three days and nights, He would return
to the "little ones" whom He had loved.

"After I have risen, I will go before you into Galilee."

After Calvary, however, hope was very thin. Hope rested
solely in that promise. Three days of hope were the only
remnants left after Good Friday, after the cross.

The counterpart of this hope was suspicion and fear.

"And on the next day the leaders of the people and
the Pharisees came to Pilate, saying: 'Lord, we have
recorded that the Seducer said while yet alive: "After

three days I will rise." Pilate therefore officially or-
dered the sepulchre to be guarded until the third
day."

The power of Naim and Capharnaum was on the one hand
trusted, and on the other feared.

The final test would be simple; it all hinged on "an empty
tomb." He had said that by His own power He would rise
again.

Now the power of God was on trial, and the verdict would
affect the life and destiny of every man who would ever
come into this world.

The hope in the hearts of those who loved Him, the fears
of those who crucified Him, would be settled beyond all
question in: an empty tomb.

*   *   *

Among the hearts broken on Mt. Calvary was that of one
Mary Magdalen.

Mary Magdalen, in worse days and better, was living proof
— as we are all living proofs — that the human heart was
made to love; made to stretch forth long, hungry arms
to find love, refusing to be denied.

It is the universal law of the human heart.

When the heart does not fasten God in its embrace, it
will lay hold of itself in one of two forms:

It will have the single eye of pride . . . or it will inhabit
the ghettos of lust.

But it will not be denied. The human heart will love at
any cost.

To understand in a kindly, sympathetic, Christlike light the
soul which has been made ugly by sin, one must understand this tremendous impulse of the heart of man:
to love.

Mary Magdalen had been a woman of the streets. No
doubt, inside and outside her hearing, she was called

cheap, degraded, a "tramp" by her self-appointed judges
who were blind to the problems of the human heart.

Her life had been a dark and lonely night of lust, until the
dawn of Jesus of Galilee broke in her life.

It was then, for the first time, that she saw through the
mist of her copious tears the pure beauty for which the
heart is made. It was then, for the first time, that she
read it in the leaves and flowers, heard it in the song
of the birds, and saw it in the face of Jesus of Galilee.

Her life opened then with her eyes; her heart felt "at
home" and the deepest instincts of that heart in her
knew it and would never doubt: this was the love that she
had sought in a million places; these were the waters of
life that now washed soothingly over her tiredness.

Her hands were cracked and bleeding from the digging,
but she had in the end found the treasure for which her
whole life had been a blind seeking.

And she had found this purest of all gifts in the hands
which she had just beheld, pierced by nails and twisting
in pain, against the sky on Mt. Calvary.

This was the Mary Magdalen who, in the deepest darkness
of the night, came to the tomb of Jesus on the morning
of the third day . . . blind to every consideration of
danger and inconvenience . . . blind to everything, perhaps, except love.

Having arrived in the little garden where Jesus had been
laid, she saw by the last rays of the moon a thing she
had never expected: the stone at the entrance of the
cave was removed, and the grave stood open.

The chill of the night air and the shock of this surprise
sent a tremor of fear through her, and in an instant she
turned back hurriedly over the moonlit road to tell the
sleeping apostles of her discovery.

"They have taken the Lord from the tomb, and we do not
know where they have laid Him," she related breathlessly.

New courage and indignation pounded in the veins of Peter
and John, as they raced to the tomb, only to find:
"... the linen cloths lying there, and the handkerchief
which had been about His head, not lying with the
linen cloths, but folded in a place by itself."
The two apostles, who had loved Jesus with every fiber of
their hearts, straightened up and their eyes met. There
was no word for there was no need for a word. Each read
it clearly and carefully in the smiling face of the other.
A thousand things were now beginning to be clear: All
that He had said . . . Yet, it was too great a thing to
have become clear and certain in a flash. But clarity and
certainty had begun to shine forth from those neatly
folded cloths.
In the distance the first bird opened his throat in song,
but the music in the hearts of the apostles swelled even
more beautifully:
Jesus had risen!
There was a new and joyous spring in their steps as they
anxiously made their way back over the road from the
tomb. Their hearts were thundering in their breasts. And
the rising of the sun in the east poured its light down
upon a new world of hope and rewarded faith.
But behind them (it must have been pure oversight) they
left a still sorrowful figure weeping in the shadows of
the garden.
Poor Mary Magdalen.
Perhaps you will pause at this place in St. John's Gospel,
as often I have, to feel a momentary sorrow for Mary.
After all, it had been Mary who, in the terrifying mo-
mentum of her overpowering love for Jesus, had run
to tell the apostles.
But when the meaning was clear . . .
When the nicely folded death wrappings announced
their solemn message, the apostles had rushed off

with brimming hearts without telling Mary, who had waited outside the cave in the shadows of the garden. Alone.

When the sun of the tremendous realization that Jesus was risen had broken through to light the worlds of Peter and John, poor Mary was left a solitary figure of grief, alone in the shadows.

But a divine plan was deeply woven into the pattern . . . hidden for the moment, but soon to reveal itself most tenderly.

For St. John tells us (the same John who had gone off with Peter):

"But Mary was standing outside weeping at the tomb. So, as she wept, she stooped down and looked into the tomb, and saw two angels in white sitting, one at the head and one at the feet, where the body of Jesus had been laid . . ."

Eyes which have done without sleep and misty with tears can be forgiven for not recognizing these white figures as citizens of another world. For it is apparent from the dialogue that Mary did not make this judgment.

"Woman, why are you weeping?"

"Because they have taken away my Lord, and I do not know where they have laid Him."

(The mother who has lost a son on some deserted and uncertain battlefield or under the vast tides of the ocean will alone fully understand the tears on Mary's cheeks . . . the grief in Mary's heart at not knowing where the body of Jesus lay.)

Then again the same question:

"Woman, why are you weeping?"

But this time the question was put by a man suddenly discovered to be standing in the garden.

"Whom do you seek?" He asked.

Mary's heart, tired and worn with grief, was in another

world . . . was back on the road where she had first seen
Jesus . . . back in the world of joy and forgiveness . . .
back into the days when she beheld Him pouring mercy
over the sick, giving sight to the blind . . . back, too,
on Calvary where He died.

If there was an otherworldly light about these figures standing guard in the black tomb, it is hardly surprising that
Mary did not see it. It is not surprising that she thought
the man in the garden was a caretaker. No wonder she
exclaimed:

"Sir, if you have removed Him, tell me where you have
laid Him and I will take Him away."

The moment had arrived. The sun was at the horizon; but
for Mary there was to be no slow-breaking dawn, no early
morning. There would suddenly and simply be a gloriously bright world. All the memories of the shadows and
the darkness would be forever gone.

It was all the warmth and the brightness of a cloudless high
noon, when:

"Jesus said to her, 'Mary'!"
"Rabboni . . . Master!"

How blessed you were, Mary, in the thoughtlessness of
Peter and John. Had you read the message of the linen
cloths you would now be back in the cenacle describing
what you had seen in that early dawn of hope. You
would not now be kissing devoutly the once-ghastly
wounds of Calvary, now transformed and shining as
brightly as the sun.

Yours was a double blessing, Mary. A blessing for yourself
and a blessing for us, for in the ecstasy of that early
morning so many years ago, in that tender reunion of
which we may now read, there is a new certainty, a new
confirmation that our trust and faith are grounded solidly
on the immovable rock of Christ's divinity.

Like you, Mary, we know that we have not believed in vain.

In the resurrection of Jesus from the dead there is an
undying pledge that someday we too shall rise again. Jesus
had promised that there would be a day when He would
come on the clouds of heaven, when He would send His
angels of judgment to cities and hinterlands of humanity
to claim His elect, to claim those who have loved Him.

On His word, we shall rise from the graves in which our
bodies shall someday rest . . . rise as He did with the scars
that the conflict has cost us shining brightly even as His
wounds . . . we have His word.

Really, Mary Magdalen did not wait alone at the mouth of
that sepulcher and tomb. The human race stood with
fixed eyes at her side. And the joy that bubbled over in
her heart at the sight of Him is the same quiet hope
which we press to our hearts, knowing that someday the
dedication of our lives to Him shall bring us that same
vision.

Christ, we know, is risen!

Chapter 4

A KINGDOM AND A CHURCH

We must go back to Christ's life, and make that life living for ourselves, by study and by prayer. At the same time, we must accept Christ as He is now living in this, our day, and in this, our world. Christ spoke often of His Kingdom, not wishing to say from the first that His work of atonement and redemption would include the institution of a new law of the Jews and their temple. The Jewish people, in anxious regard for their own religion, their law and their temple, would certainly have put Christ to death had He been bold and direct from the beginning. It is true that He was their Messias, but time and human imagination had distorted the descriptions of the prophecies. Instead of the Messias they had been told by the prophets to expect, they had taken to looking for a temporal, political, and material Messias. The beatitudes of Christ, which would bless poverty, meekness, and suffering, were hardly a part of their anticipation. Gradually, then, in the face of such preconceptions and prejudices, Christ founded His Church, the living voice of His teaching, the living perpetuation of His mission among men. Withstanding all the disorders and attacks to which human organizations are subject, His Church has endured the trials and tribulations of twenty centuries, producing for God's world thousands of saints, and growing with an increase which finds explanation only in the favor and protection of almighty God. Christ's Church has for these long years remained steadfast in her protection of His teachings, refusing compromise, refusing to modernize the truths which Christ taught and championed. She has offered the world the countless fruits of her divine enterprise, and she remains confident in her role in the drama of human salvation, because Christ has promised her:

> "I will be with you all days, even unto the consummation of the world."

> The skeptic Ernest Renan, once said: "A thousand times more loving, a thousand times more beloved since His death than during the days He passed upon the earth, Jesus Christ has become to such a degree the cornerstone of humanity that to take away His name from the world would be to shake it to its foundations."

And yet . . .

There will always be Capharnaum . . . There will always be Naim and Bethany.

There will always be an empty tomb, and the neatly folded wrappings of death.

There will always be the sick, the sightless, and the unclean — given health and vision and cleanness through words with hidden power, through soft, transforming touches of an almighty hand.

And these will forever be beacons throwing a brilliant light from a tower twenty centuries distant: through the years in an almost endless succession: 1959 . . . 1969 . . . 1979 . . . 1989 . . .

And when the great sound of Gabriel's trumpet startles our
distracted human race, on some unknown future day,
that light shall be shining just as surely as the sun.

The last man, on that last day, will — if only he chooses —
read the why and the wherefore by the brilliance of that
light of Christ shining out of the ancient past.

The light that was life . . . the light that is the light of
the world.

Each of us shall someday be ushered from the stage of this
life, through the inevitable exit of death and we shall each
be judged in that light, judged to be worthy to live
eternally in the land of light, or . . . destined to the
doom and damnation of our choosing.

"For as the lightning comes forth from the east and
shines even to the west, so also will the coming of
the Son of Man be . . . And then will appear the sign
of the Son of Man in heaven; and then will all
tribes of the earth mourn, and they will see the Son
of Man coming upon the clouds of heaven with great
power and majesty. And He will send forth His angels
with a trumpet and a great sound, and they will
gather His elect from the four winds, from one end
of the heavens to the other" (Mt. 24:28–31).

And so we must go back, now, back to Capharnaum, to
Naim and Bethany . . . back to the source of light, and
the source of life.

For one who would give his sincere mind
to the study of Christ's life and person
the way ahead is challenging. It is not easy
nor always delightful to study, read, and
pray about Christ. But Christ never promised ease in this life. In fact, it is the cross
that symbolizes Christ. One thing, however,

Christ's follower will certainly possess: life
eternal.

Despite the lure of the golf course, the bridge club, and
the bowling league (not to mention the movies and television) . . . despite the fact that the leisure to think and
read and pray is not apparent . . .

We must make reasonable concessions to demands upon
our time, but this, this we must demand:

We must demand of ourselves the strength and determination to pray . . . to say No without com-
promising when some new fascination would rob us
of the time we have marked off ". . . for God."

We must demand of ourselves a promise not to turn back,
when the journey back to Christ seems too long or too
unrewarding.

We must demand time.

Time is of the essence.

For it takes time to ponder the Gospels, to understand the
import and meaning of Christ in our lives, to see the
appeal of Christ, to be moved by the persuasions of His
proofs.

It takes time and prayer for the heart to feel the thrill of
power, the impact and the realization of the divine; time
to know and to live and love and . . . to find God's
comforts.

It is so necessary that we take our tired hearts back to
Christ . . . that we sit on the hillside and eat bread and
fishes with the multitude . . . to sit with Christ at Jacob's
well in Samaria, and listen to words which promise
"living water" . . . to see bandaged Lazarus walking from
his tomb after four days of death . . . to live over again
these scenes.

We must above all stand at the foot of the cross . . . upon
which the world was redeemed . . . and wait with Mary
Magdalen in the garden of resurrection.

We must take up the Gospels then . . . read them . . . live
them . . . study them . . . and pray over every line.

As you are reading these poor lines, the watch at your wrist
or the clock on your kitchen wall is ticking away the
seconds. To you these are vital seconds . . . seconds not
to be wasted.

There is a stranger at your door . . . There is a question to
be answered.

*   *   *

> While it is altogether necessary that we
> learn Christ from the Gospels, as He was
> then, it is equally vital that we meet Christ
> in our own day as He is now, here and
> among us. Christ's Kingdom and Christ in
> His Kingdom are very much a part of our
> daily living. We turn now to a considera-
> tion of the Kingdom of Christ in its his-
> torical setting.

At the same time . . .

The Kingdom of Christ is not a tower of the past . . .
fallen.

> Nor a fire of devout enthusiasm burnt out . . . cold
> ashes.

> Nor the arc of a flame in the sky . . . a meteoric
> moment.

No, none of these, because:

> "I will be with you all days, even unto the consumma-
> tion of the world!"

The Kingdom of Christ was then and was there.

But the Kingdom is also now and here.

It will always be even until the consummation of the world,
when the love which binds men to Christ becomes an
eternal bond, when the Kingdom of time becomes a Kingdom of eternity.

"Do not lay up for yourselves," He said, "treasures on earth,
where rust and moth consume, and where thieves break
in and steal; but lay up for yourselves treasures in heaven,
where neither rust nor moth consumes, nor thieves break
in and steal. For where thy treasure is, there also will thy
heart be."

Here is the Kingdom in our midst, teaching us to spurn the
lure of earthly treasure, teaching us to love the eternal.

No, this Kingdom of Christ is not a thing of historical
record, buried in the intellectual and spiritual debris of
2000 years. It is a thing of flesh and blood, and grace and
life.

It is just as much now as it was then:
A reason to live and a reason to die.

This Kingdom of Christ is alive in every city and village of
the world, where there is a soul given to the love of
Christ. It pulsates even where there are no homes . . . on
the paved highways and the mud roads of the world.

It is an arrow of light into the darkest regions of human
existence.

It does not come alive with each dawn . . . as though the
world of the spirit has a dawn and a dusk. The life of
grace, the love of Christ is timeless.

The Kingdom, too, is timeless, placeless: wherever the life
of baptism and full belief in Christ is lived, professed —
wherever there are men marching in the ranks of Christ,
stepping to the beat of Christ's drums — there is the
Kingdom.

*   *   *

In the face of antipathy, disbelief, and the narrowness of
prejudice, Christ did not speak of all this boldly and
clearly from the first.

Gradually He put rock upon rock and when the building
was finally completed, it was clear: He had come to estab-

lish a new order, a new economy of salvation. He had
come to initiate a Kingdom.

In the beginning there was only a vague design, a pencil
sketching. The Jews had felt a certain arrogance about
their law, and the Scribes and Pharisees guarded every
letter of that law with a self-righteous rigidity and a
jealousy that earned for them Christ's terrible words:
"whitened sepulchres!"

In the thinking and in the dreams of the Jews was a haunt-
ing anticipation: the Messias. How incredulous they would
have been if the "carpenter's son" had told them the
stark truth immediately as He had told the woman at
Jacob's well: "I with whom you speak am He."

Their dreams were of a Messias of sword and flame, marching gallantly at the head of richly arrayed armies, a Messias of conquest and opulence . . .

Certainly not a Messias who would take poverty by the
hand, and tell His people: Here is your queen . . . love
her and honor her . . . Blessed are the poor in spirit . . .
Blessed are the peacemakers . . . Blessed are the clean
of heart.

Had Christ, the Messias of the spirit, met their granite
preconceptions head-on, had He revealed Himself and
unveiled His new economy of grace and redemption too
hastily . . . Calvary would not have waited; death would
have been as inevitable as it would have been immediate.

And so, He did not pour out at once the new mercies for
men which He came bearing in His divine hands; a new
law of love to replace the old law of exterior conformity,
of an eye for an eye and a tooth for a tooth.

To those who perceived, when their minds broke through
the veiled imagery and the parables, He had said: (because they knew what He was about) —

"Blessed are your eyes, for they see; and your ears, for
they hear. For amen I say to you, many prophets

and just men have longed to see what you see, and
they have not seen it; and to hear what you hear,
and they have not heard it."

Jesus likened His Kingdom to a man who sowed good seed
in his field, as also to a mustard seed and a net cast into
the sea. Why?

The Jews were a highly imaginative people with three-
dimensional minds, not too fond nor too capable of
abstract speculation. A field of grain, a mustard seed, a
net cast into the sea: there was here something a man
can see and touch and smell.

So Christ spoke their language. They perhaps could not
have grasped the paradox of the Kingdom of God having
the good and the bad in its embrace nor the notions of
separation, reward, and punishment . . . much more easily
could they get the notion of "a man who sowed good
seed and whose enemies sowed weeds along with the
good seed." Much more easily could they see a net being
plunged into the sea, bringing up worthy fish and the
unworthy which will be thrown back.

In the parables Christ let the truth seep through to them.
"The Kingdom of Heaven is likened to a mustard seed.
. . . This is indeed the smallest of all the seeds; but
when it grows up it is larger than any herb and
becomes a tree, so that the birds of the air come
and dwell in its branches."
. . . So it would be: He would start with a handful
of disciples, a very small beginning, but the Kingdom will be born; and from this smallest of seeds,
it shall grow enormously. It shall be:
. . . a leaven . . . a treasure hidden in a field . . . a
net cast into the sea.

The final masterpiece took form only gradually. Each stroke
of the divine artist's brush added a new line of beauty
and clarity.

Here was the Light of this world appearing to men, reveal-
ing to men, according to the capacities of men, gradually
and gently like the diffusing light of the rising sun.
Slowly, but surely, the Kingdom was revealed.

Slowly but surely: "Thou art Peter, and upon this rock, I
shall build My Church."

Ah! this is it: His Church.

Calvary would not be enough. Calvary would heal the
bleeding wound of Adam. Calvary would open the
bolted doors of heaven . . .

But to save all men, the merits of His death on the cross
would have to be applied, channeled to the souls of men.
He must die to save men, and yet:
He must live to save men.

He must live on, in His Kingdom, in His Church, in order
that He might breathe His life into men.

What a mercy this mercy of God: to channel a participation in His divine life into the hearts and souls of men,
to pour lavishly a sharing of the divine into the human
receptacle . . .

Through His Church: great channels of life, of strength, of
forgiveness.

The reservoir of Christ's divine wealth so lavishly given to
men is not to be measured. Man does not plunge his
puny yardsticks to sound the depths of infinity.

There shall be, by His coming, abundant life, abundant
strength, and abundant forgiveness for all men, in all
times . . . wherever there is an open heart.

But men must drink, must seize upon these channels of
life, strength, and forgiveness.

There is in the living Kingdom of God a wealth of God's
life for the taking, but a man must take.

We do not gain God's strength and life and forgiveness
from the air about us nor from the imagination within
us. The channels at which we drink must be God's

channels. And so it is of the highest importance for
men to know:
  where God's channels are!

> There can be no human reasons for a
> divine action. We cannot impute human
> motives to God. His ways are simply not
> our ways. Still God deals with us, and
> might I say, works with us as human
> beings. Mysterious human psychology is no
> mystery to the Maker of human nature.
> With the words of Christ and the needs
> of human nature, then, as our guide, we
> look into the purpose of Christ in found-
> ing a Kingdom here in this world.

Christ the eternal stranger at the doors of the world, did
  not come only to redeem, to give life. Christ came to
  teach, to teach man the mind of God.
He did not take human form only to teach a small class
  of students in ancient Palestine — the majority of that
  class would fail in the final test, anyway.
Christ came to teach all men. Christ came to teach you
  and me.
He poured the wisdom of God into the ears of twelve men.
What I have whispered into your ears, He enjoined, shout
  from the housetops.
  "He who hears you hears Me!"
  "Shout what I have told you down the centuries. Be
    the unfaltering, living voice of 'My Church!'"
  "The gates of Hell shall not prevail against it."
Under the inspiration of the Holy Spirit, Matthew, Mark,
  Luke, and John would write down some of His teachings
  in their Gospels. But . . .

A book without a teacher is not enough.

There must be, according to divine wisdom:

"The Church of the living God . . . the pillar and mainstay of truth!"

A book, we know, can be misinterpreted.

The lines of print can become vague and shadowy, and you and I can wander down the darkened labyrinths of our and understanding, and into tragedy.

There must be a living voice to guide us, to hold us in the right way, to take us by the hand when we would walk from the beaten path into the treacherous jungles of personal, subjective thinking.

There must be a teacher to whom we are responsible.

"If he refuses to hear the Church, let him be to thee as the heathen and the publican . . ."

Oh, certainly there was a textbook, and a good one. The writings of the four, and the letters of Peter, John, and Paul. These wrote what God wanted and because God wanted, and nothing which God did not want.

Still, there was never anywhere a command of Christ to write.

The command was: to "preach and teach . . ."

Nowhere to write . . . Christ did not call them to be secretaries.

Christ called them to be a "living voice . . ." to be heard till the ends of time.

"I will be with you all days, even till the consummation of the world."

A consideration of the role of the Kingdom or Church and the New Testament; the role of the Church and its necessity for salvation.

The life of God is offered to every man.

The living voice of His teaching would be heard till the last echo from the side of the mountain fades into eternal silence on the last day.

"Of His Kingdom there shall be no end."

The living teacher would perpetuate in life all His works.

The Church built upon the rock of Peter would use the textbook of the New Testament, but the textbook would belong to the teacher, would be produced by the teaching Church.

It is not contrariwise: The teacher does not belong to the book, nor is the teacher produced by the book.

Christ's Church would be charged with the authority of heaven; with the authority of Christ Himself:

to teach, to forgive the sins of men, to sanctify the lives of men.

And necessarily so.

For Christ wished His Church to be Himself, a continuation of Himself and His mission. Only this desire of Christ makes any sense out of his question to Saul, who was a vicious attacker of the infant Church: "Why do you persecute Me?" ". . . Me?" Christ asked of the man who had never before seen Christ.

Christ wished the temple of His Church to withstand the rumblings of the earth, the battering rains, the gusts and the gales of time.

Christ wanted His Church to be a sturdy shelter for the wayfaring sons of Adam and the daughters of Eve.

Oh, this Church would come upon Calvaries of its own, and bleed just as its divine founder and inspiration bled and knew His Calvary.

Yet His Church would be another Christ.

She would speak as "one having authority" just as this was said of Christ's own speech so truly.

She would be confident that in her words was a divine sure-

ness . . . a divine support. Christ would Himself live in
her, guide her destinies, because from the beginning the
whole enterprise was His:
   "As the Father has sent Me . . . so I send you."

                *   *   *

"The weak things of this earth God has chosen to con-
   found the strong."
Twelve men . . . handpicked by eternal wisdom . . . chosen
   to launch the great ark of salvation . . . endowed with
   powers that would prostrate the angels with awe . . .
   commissioned to reach every nation . . . custodians of
   the word of God . . . protected in their message by the
   promise of God Himself.
Yet, we must not forget, these were men . . . capable of
   misery and cowardice . . . capable of high treason to the
   highest cause of God . . . human blood was in their
   veins, and human fears in their hearts.
These were the chosen instruments of God.
And in their selection, in their commission: A Church.
Men may find their way to heaven without embracing that
   Church, but only if they do not know, only if their eyes
   are innocently shut and their hearts are good.
But even then: ignorance is not the price or merit of their
   salvation. Ignorance is a negative thing, a privation of
   truth. Ignorance is not the food of eternal life. Those
   who are in such ignorance will live by the food falling
   from the table of Christ's Church.
They will live by belief in the truths which Christ's Church
   has kept sacred and intact.
      "Whoever will believe will be saved . . . who will not
      believe will be condemned."
The Church of Christ: a fortress in the desert storm. Some
   are saved in the wake of the winds, not because they
   were within the fortress of the Church, but because they

huddled closely against the protection of her outer walls.
The Church of Christ: an ark in the flood. Some will not
drown, not because they were aboard the ark of the
Church, but only because they clutched to floating timber which fell from the decks of the ark.

"Whoever will believe will be saved . . . who will not
believe will be condemned."

*   *   *

If Christ really lives today in His Church,
and if Christ is really God, then there must
be a Church which can alone claim the
finger of God in its origins and history.
This Church is not twenty centuries away
from Christ, but has been living twenty
centuries with Christ; or better, He has
lived in His Church for twenty centuries.
Looking at the life and words of Christ,
we would expect these marks to distinguish
His Church: Holiness — Growth beyond
human explanation — Unity in truth, worship, and obedience — and a Stability in
the face of persecution from without and
sickness from within. These marks can
belong only to the church which God
blesses and in which God lives, for these
are achievements beyond human capacity.
A man may find that these marks lead
him to a door he has studiously shunned
because he has hated the name above that
door. But his hatred and prejudice will die
quickly if he is convinced that this is
where God lives. There follows a consideration of these divine earmarks and the
Roman Catholic Church.

The finger of God . . . an indelible imprint of divine
approval, divine life.

Twelve stumbling, stuttering fishermen, taken from their
boats and nets to be made "fishers of men." They are
almost incorrigible in their belief that Christ's empire is
to be a worldly empire to rival Rome. They are stupidly
persistent in their desire to be "first" in His Kingdom of
material power . . .

These twelve were given a charter:

"All power in heaven and on earth has been given to
Me. Go therefore and make disciples of all nations,
baptizing them in the name of the Father, and of
the Son, and of the Holy Spirit, teaching them to
observe all that I have commanded you; and behold
I am with you all days, even unto the consummation
of the world."

These twelve fishermen took this charter and took the
divine fire into their hands . . . hands which reeked of
fish . . . and they threw the flames forth to all men.

Ten of the twelve gave the scarlet testimony of their
blood. They poured that blood into the ground as though
it were waste . . . and the seeds of a thousand Christians
broke through that ground almost at once . . . and the
more they were eradicated in the Roman arenas, on the
burning crosses, by the mouths of the hungry lions, the
more gloriously did they multiply.

This divine fire would not be extinguished!

"Behold, I am with you all days, even unto the consummation of the world!"

Christ present in His Church . . . working a thousand
miracles in the souls of men . . . bringing a countless
host of hearts to the dedication of love . . . setting afire
the souls of men to endure every form of anguish, echo-
ing the cry of St. Paul: "It is the love of Christ that
drives me on!"

Christ present in His Church . . . bringing inspiration to
hands and hearts weary with the struggle . . . giving birth
to a thousand accomplishments, undertaken solely for
His love . . . making great men with great hearts . . .
asking much . . . receiving more.

Christ present in His Church . . . in the Roman dungeons
. . . in the distant reaches of barbarian lands . . . in human
hands that wash the wounds of the lepers . . . in eyes that
flash hope and love and kindness when the tongue has
been cut away for whispering His name . . .

Christ present in His Church . . . in countless thousands of
consecrated souls who have lain willingly and joyfully on
the fires of sacrifice . . . who have made an oblation of
their most natural, most ingrained instincts . . . who give
and do not count the cost . . . who labor till all their
energy is poured out asking only for the reward of His
love . . .

Christ present in His Church . . . Holding steadfastly to
the teachings of Christ, when others have protested and
departed to try the truth of Infinite Wisdom in the dimly
lit courts of human intelligence . . . keeping the sanctity
of the home and of marriage inviolable when others have
bowed to convention . . . Christ present in His Church
which is almost alone His champion and defender.

Christ present in His Church . . . preserving the goods of
justice and charity . . . raising high the torch of chastity
. . . keeping the values of men in line with the values
of God.

If Renan was right — "Jesus Christ has become to such a
degree the cornerstone of humanity that to take away
His name from the world would be to shake it to its
foundations . . ."

Then we can also say: Remove Christ's Church and you
remove the only certainty in an uncertain world. Remove
Christ's Church and you take away the only object of

trust in a world of mistrust. Remove Christ's Church and you take away from an insane world the only guarantee of sanity. Remove Christ's Church and the voice of God will be silent forever.

If, indeed, we were to remove the Church, back we would go to the law of the jungle, where size and might are the standards of truth and where wrong is a lack of animal cunning.

It is reassuring to know that such a day will never be, for: "Behold I am with you all days, even unto the consummation of the world . . ."

Christ shall live on and always be present in His Church . . . holding out to men only His cross . . . meeting men's minds undisguised in demands . . . yet marked by a growth too grand to be mistaken. Man waters, but God gives the increase. From a handful: a perpetual springtime of bud and blossom and blade of new life. In three hundred years five million new Christians . . . and in these first three hundred years the price of Christianity was perpetual risk of one's life . . . But the Christian's cry was a cry of Christ's triumph:

"We are but of yesterday, and yet we have filled every place among you — cities, islands, fortresses, towns, market places, camp, tribes, town councils, the palace, the senate, the forum; we have left nothing to you but the temples of your gods . . . Even unarmed and without any uprising, merely as malcontents, simply through hatred and withdrawal, we could have fought against you. For if such a multitude of men as we are had broken loose from you and had gone into some remote corner of the earth, the loss of so many citizens would certainly have made your power blush for shame . . . You would have been exceedingly frightened at your loneliness, at the silence of your surroundings, and the stupor, as it were, of a dead world. You would have had to look around for people to rule; there would have been more enemies than citizens left to you . . ." (From Tertullian's *Apology*).

This was the brag of a Christian only one hundred and fifty years after the Son of Man had said: "Thou art Peter, and upon this rock I shall build My Church."

This growth was God's growth, God's gift.

Things which are essentially dissimilar cannot be added: a man and a tree are not counted as two something.

And yet, to violate the rule, add these dissimilars together: A Church founded by a son of the most despised of races . . . the son of a "carpenter" in a village the name and location of which were hidden by the shadows of a nearby mountain. A Church whose first priests and preachers were timid and ignorant Jews, thick-tongued and thick-headed until the Divine Tongues of Fire on Pentecost. A Church to champion chastity, monogamy, meekness, and charity, all rugged doctrines . . . A Church to be diffused through veins which were stopped up with prejudice and the anticipation of a Napoleonic Messias . . . through a paganism rigidly frozen: this was to be a springtime. A Church spreading wildly on the force of love for One Man and One Ideal. A Church poised and confident under the snarl of Rome's divine despots . . . A Church opposed at every turn, driven to the wall, gouged and clawed and burned . . .

Now add these things together. What did you get?

The sum is, according to Euclid: Defeat . . . annihilation!

But we check the answer book of history. There the factual answer reads: wild, unextinguishable growth. A unique phenomenon in its propagation. Without parallel in the story of man. Since Adam, there is no story with the grip, the pathos, the drama of this . . . Psychologically, all was against it. For this to succeed too much of the impossible was necessary.

When you check this against the unbelievable success story of the fortunes of this Church, there is no doubt.

A hopelessly lost cause succeeds with grandiose success. Here is the mark of the divine; here is the finger of God: the answer of God to the Christian prayer:

"Thy Kingdom come . . ."

The answer to the prayer of Christ to His Father at the Last Supper:

"Yet not for these only do I pray, but for those also who through their word are to believe in Me, that all may be one, even as Thou, Father, in Me and I in Thee; that they also may be one in Us, that the world may believe that Thou hast sent Me . . . that Thou hast loved them even as Thou hast loved Me."

Christ is present in His Church in still another way: in the oneness and unity of truth, in oneness of worship, oneness in the surrender of man's dearest liberty, the surrender to conform, in spite of the autonomy which is so natural and so precious to man. Here are these millions surrendering happily their sovereignty to seek surety in submission, and to merit an eternal reward.

Never could a human enterprise achieve this. Here we look at a unique phenomenon. Here we behold the hand of God. Here we see realized: "I will be with you all days . . ."

All days . . . even down through the long years of buffeting storms, storms enough to reface the earth . . . storms of sickness and revolution within: the sorrowing sons who have abandoned Christ's house, their home . . . the violent fists of iron constantly throbbing in anger at her door . . . Indeed, a vanguard, so mighty in mind and matter; politically potent to destroy any natural foe . . . drawing blood . . . yet afraid at the sight:

This Church, covered with the blood of attack, staggering and almost falling . . . is, of all things, smiling

and confident . . . looking out to the ends of the
world . . . in apparent defeat and yet planning new
conquests, because: "I will be with you all days . . ."
The Church of Christ, in all her preaching, in all her teaching, has never claimed to possess all human knowledge,
nor does she canonize her total membership. The net
cast into the sea will bring in both the good and the bad
fish . . . the good wheat and the weeds will thrive side
by side. There will be dead wood, lifeless branches on
the tree. Even regarding those who have stood in the
place of Peter, James, and John, history will have many
sad chapters . . . the mothering Church will weep for
her wayward sons, who have gone astray in spite of her
maternal love and care.
But for all the tarnish, for all the tinsel that should have
been gold, the mother is not to be blamed. She will
always, just as she has always, say and know that she is
divine because a divine hand guides her destinies, just
as a divine will gave her life: "I will be with you all
days . . ."
Men may leave her sanctuary, and say that she is not a
good mother, and even protest to other men that their
mother has failed in holiness.
But this is not what they really mean to say.
They really mean that some of her children have not been
worthy of their mother. This is a human experience that
few have not encountered. We would not think of blam-
ing the mother whose son has disgraced her in spite of
her heroic efforts and the sacrifices she has made to help
and train that son.
In the sixteenth century some few disowned their mother,
the Catholic Church. They took millions more with them
away from this mother.
They rather meant to disown the evil in some of her
sons . . . but the shaft missed its mark sadly. Their

mother's purity was unblemished: from her immaculate womb she was bearing many heroic souls: Rodriguez . . . Avellino . . . Merici . . . Realino . . . Cajetan . . . Casimir . . . Catherine de Ricci . . . Catherine of Genoa . . . Charles Borromeo . . . Francis Borgia . . . Francis Xavier . . . Ignatius Loyola . . . James Kisai . . . Jerome Emilian . . . John Fisher . . . John of the Cross . . . Peter Canisius . . . Robert Bellarmine . . . Teresa of Avila . . . Thomas More.

Had they but stayed in the arms of their mother, among these canonized saints of their time might be numbered the names of Martin Luther, King Henry VIII of England, and John Calvin. If only they had placed more confidence in the necessary holiness of their mother. If only they had realized more deeply and more imperturbably and more humbly:

". . . upon this rock I shall build My Church, and the gates of Hell shall not prevail against it!"

It is a sad thing to see a man walk out of his mother's house and from his Father's love with bitterness in his heart. The mother continues to whisper her continual prayers for these sons who have left her in such bitterness, that they may realize what a great lonesomeness has come into their lives and eagerly seek the road back home.

* * *

Christ's Church, like her divine Founder, would also have her Calvaries. Like Him she will know what it is to bleed, to be misunderstood and rejected and hated. She will suffer defections from within in her moment of agony. For her as for Christ there will be a thousand other Gardens of Olives . . . a thousand crowns of thorns. She will feel the inner sickness of her Founder's agony, and will herself sweat blood.

But — and this is all important — in one thing she will not be like her Master:

She will never die!

She will live on gloriously surmounting the mighty boulders and the fallen oaks in her path of progress. She will be unafraid even in her darkest hours, when the sky is opaque and the earth is trembling under her feet. The bright sunshine of confidence is forever in her heart, for over that heart she wears a promise, wears the word of her divine Lord and Master:

"Behold I am with you all days, even unto the consummation of the world!"

Chapter 5

"MY CHURCH"

It is a byword with the reasonably pious that man has a basic need for *religion*. The need for religion is, I think, just another way of saying that man has a psychological need for God. But it is more than just this. The mind of man is made to hold God's truth and the heart of man, as Augustine says, does not rest till it rests in God.

At one time or another each of us turns to God with a fervor we did not think was in us. We clutch God in these moments almost as though we had never known Him before. But our emotions desert us in a short while, they wear out, and God's vivid presence fades like a star that has shone in the sky for one night only. Our fits of fervor do not yield enough strength for our day by day service of almighty God. We need help. As human, social beings we need a church. We need to kneel down with the men who live about us and to pray as a member of a group. The sense and strength of numbers is in our nature. We need the feeling and support of corporate worship. We need the example of others. We need heroes we can admire and seek to imitate.

Just *any* church is a fallacy and foolishness, if Christ founded one Church. Though a man may wait for a long time on the threshold, torn by doubts and indecision, the course of entrance will eventually be clear to him if his mind is open and his heart is strong with courage.

If he is determined, the grace of God will work in and through him. If he is determined, without a doubt he will find Christ!

You and I seek shelter.

But we need more than a roof, food, and a garment. Brute beasts have need for these.

But you and I are not mere living things that feel the bite of a winter wind and the pangs of hunger in the pits of our stomachs. There is another hunger in us, a hunger in the deepest pits of our hearts.

The ability to think and desire, as humans think and desire, creates in us a thousand needs of mind and heart; at times a dire loneliness, a need to love and a need to be loved . . . a painful need to know what is right and what is wrong, what is really true and good and beautiful.

This is at once the price and the privilege of being human.

The heart is anxious that the mind should find truth. The heart does not rest until the mind finds truth, and the heart can have its own share of the reward.

This, for most men, is a sweaty turmoil, and there are a thousand blind alleys . . . and human nausea in the human heart at the point of failure.

The need for security is a great need; it is the need for truth.

Truth contents the mind, stimulates the weary heart.

A man may not yet have worked out the theory, may not have settled upon the formula, but his grasping for truth, and the happiness that comes with truth, begins with his alarm clock in the morning and ends with the end of his day. He may not even realize.

We count the crimes of our society, and recount the

cruelties and malices of which the human heart has been found capable. We throw up our hands, and curse self-righteously, even though the same seeds of malice lie fermenting in our own fibers.

When these seeds of evil in us give painful evidence of being alive, and there is no finer thing in our life to keep us inspired, to keep us in love with life, we seek refuge. You and I seek shelter.

We feel drawn to abandon ourselves to a wickedness of one sort or other: to lust, drink, dope, or despair.

Or . . .

We turn to God.

We turn to seek the meaning of life from the maker of life. This moment of communion with God may send tears down the cheeks, may cause bitter compunction or warm peace in the heart, or even leave the heart a stone, but:

A soundless voice gives us this assurance: it is the right thing.

Let's name it with its right name: In our desperation, we become *religious*.

It is not a mask we wear, not a sedative to put our painful desires to sleep. There is no suggestion of hypocrisy. No man has to apologize for leaning on God. In fact, some lean on God because it is fashionable and not because they are helpless creatures.

For us there is a newness about God in this finding of Him. A new realization.

It may be that this new finding of God will be a star that shines in the sky for one night only. We shall search and search the sky thereafter to look for a renewal of its comfort and realization, but the sky is jet . . .

And the heart is jet.

And it is no wonder.

Ideas of the mind die, unless . . . unless we take them out

of the mind, and put them into our daily lives. A man
cannot *think* religiously for long, if he does not live
religiously.

A man cannot say to God:
I have found You . . . I shall never unlock my arms.
If he does not find God also in daily honesty,
daily generosity, daily worship.

Man is not made that way.

Man is not made to live a contradiction: to think and feel
and love one way, and live another.

Our dear finding of God must be nourished . . . or it will
die.

But we sense this, do we not? So we live religiously. We
choke back that cutting word, silence the urges of our
flesh, try to balance the scales of justice, and at day's
end, we say our good night and our thanks to God.

But in the shock of daily battle the desire becomes thinner
and thinner.

Our neighbor does not share our enthusiasm for the scales
of justice; the neighbor throttles us with sharp and
wounding words.
And, this, to be sure, does not help.

We cannot travel alone.

The social instinct in us looks for companionship in this
long and difficult journey. Our good night to God does
not fan the flame enough to keep it alive.

We need a Church, an organization.

We know that our enthusiasm for bridge would have died
without the Bridge Club. We know that our interest
in bowling is kept alive by the Wednesday Night Bowling League.

So our enthusiasm for God will die a gradual death without some organization, some league, some Church . . .

It is very simple. Man is made that way.

* * *

Did God, in making man a social being
and in foreseeing this need for man to be
identified with a religious group, wish that
there be one Church or is any church acceptable in God's eyes? The answer perhaps
lies in the words of Christ and our limited
knowledge of the nature and will of God,
our Father.

A kindly old soul with a gentle passion to live and let live
once was heard to say:
"All religions are ways to the same destination. It
doesn't matter which road you follow; all rivers lead
to the ocean and all churches bring you to the same
place."
It was a bland saying, bore in its connotation a spirit of
tolerance, graciousness, and broad-mindedness. When a
man said it in one version or another, he felt expansive.
Soon it became a household saying, the badge of largeness
. . . it became a philosophy that a man was proud to
display, like the blossom in his coat lapel.
There is a mild and sweet fragrance from this flower.
It remained quite beside the point that the saying was not
true, and that the fragrance it breathed forth was the
fragrance of chloroform . . . intellectual chloroform which
will mildly and painlessly put the mind to sleep, and lull
a man away from the great and true conviction that
Christ wanted one Church.
A Church is not a thing which we shop for . . . like a neck-
tie or a pocketbook.
Two thousand years ago, Christ built a Church.
He said solemnly: ". . . and the gates of Hell shall not
prevail against it . . . for behold, I will be with you all
days, even to the consummation of the world."

Somewhere the Church of Christ is still standing . . . And
   Christ is standing with that Church . . . And the peace
   which Christ promised to men are the goods of that
   Church.
   "Even unto the consummation of the world."
Christ spoke of:
   "THE Church . . . MY Church . . ."
He did not say Churches.
He did say that there would be ONE fold and ONE
   shepherd.
He did say that a house divided against itself will not stand.
He did pray to His Father at the Last Supper that all His
   followers "may be one even as We are one."
Dynamic St. Paul, offering always the sole credential and
   authority of "an apostle of Jesus Christ," told the
   Ephesians: "I exhort you to walk in a manner worthy
   of the calling with which you were called, carefully to
   preserve the unity of the Spirit in the bond of peace:
   one body and one spirit, even as you were called in one
   hope of your calling; One Lord, one faith, one baptism."
The fact is this: There are not many rivers all leading to
   the ocean . . . there are not many roads leading to the
   same destination.
The fact is that "He who is not with Me is against Me."
Truth is above all one.
Besides the words of the Scriptures . . .
Think of this: the God who made this world, who made
   the mind and heart of man, the God of the sun and
   moon . . .
      He is a God of harmony.
The astronomer finds this harmony in countless heavenly
   bodies swimming in precise orbits through God's magnificent skies. The scientist finds harmony in the order of
   the atom. The physician in the cellular functions of the
   body.

Take up a leaf from any tree. Study the symmetry in its veins.

Take up a flower. Look at the exquisite harmony and order of the petals.

God's harmony is one great swell of order, in the skies, in the gardens, in the fields.

Now put this question to yourself:

> Does this God, looking down upon the children of His heart, this human family of His . . . does He say:
>
> > "But in worshipping Me, let there be plentiful division and disagreement!"?

Does God say to us: "I am best served by differences and rifts, by doubt and divergence in doctrine. If you would love Me, begin debating"?

God no more says this than the teacher who assigns the problem in arithmetic assures her class:

> "I want a great variety of answers."
>
> She wants One answer, the correct answer.

God wants "One fold and One shepherd."

If the Gospels do not say it clearly enough, your own reasoning will:

> God wants One Church and One faith.

Besides the all-important word of Christ, we have a logic which alone seems worthy of our great God, whose first law is order and harmony and unity.

> The unity of which Christ spoke and to which reason itself leads us is found in only one Church, the Roman Catholic Church. A man might be bitter in his view of the Catholic Church, but if he is honest he will see and admit that outside that Church, faith is not one and the unity Christ prayed for is chaos. But there is this

objection: Any Church could achieve this
unity by imposing dogmas . . . any Church
could achieve attendance by threatening
mortal sin. I do not want to be told what
to do, what to believe. I do not want to
be a Roman Catholic parrot.
There follows a consideration of these
difficulties.

To very many the words "Roman Catholic" represent a
hard saying.
  And the connotations are hard.
And yet, beyond the high and sturdy fences of this hard
saying . . . outside this house, whatever we think of its
timber and architecture . . . there is no united Christianity, and so there is no authentic Christianity. There is
no Christianity where there is disunity.
But even more telling: There is no promise, no rule, no
guarantee, and no hope of there ever being a united and
therefore true Christianity outside of the Catholic Church
. . . that united and true Christianity for which the Son
of God prayed: ". . . that they may be one even as You
and I are one . . ."
Let us be honest. Let us admit that all men, you and I
included, want to choose our beliefs with the same sover-
eign independence that we choose to be Democrat or
Republican or fans of the Los Angeles Dodgers.
We want. That is for sure, we want.
But wants are like so many other impulses in us. Like
ungovernable children, who need to be tamed . . . riotous
whims that must be shorn and subjected.
For example, you may want: to remain in bed each day
till late afternoon . . . to be a king or a queen and to sit
on the shoulders of other men . . . to kill a man or covet
his wife.

But the mind in you, the grim honesty and the unsilenced
voice of your conscience, and the sanctions that men mete
out for crime—these bring you to your senses. You
realize that it is not reasonable to be governed by wants.
When we indulge indiscriminately in wanting, we call these
whims our "pipe dreams."
They are "pipe dreams" because they do not grow in the
dirt of what we know is honest and real.
This, for example, would be a "pipe dream."

> To say to God: "I will try You at the bar of my
> reason. I will hear Your case personally. My desires
> will sit in jury upon You."
> To say to God: "There is for You no court of appeal
> higher than these: my reason and my desires."

These are "pipe dreams."
We have, if we have said these things in our hearts to
God, run away like child cowards from what we know
is honest and real. We have become spoiled children,
little tyrants who threaten God that we will take up our
toys and go home, unless He plays the game as we wish it.
We have—when we begin to suit God's law to our whims
—fitted God comfortably into our lives, allotted Him
just so much of our time, just so much of our heart.
God has been made to meet our plans. We have com-
mitted the highest crime of irrationality: we have made
the creator the creature.
A man might despise or ignore the Roman Catholic voice,
because . . . well, because it is too dogmatic; it is a
voice too sure and too confident. It speaks with all the
authority of Him who "spoke as one having authority,"
who said to His Church: "He who hears you, hears Me."
We sit back in the imagined luxury of our self-made mon-
archies . . . the unruled and forbidden desires of our
hearts sit as children in our laps. They are as close to us
as the soft and warm flesh that covers our bones.

We hold these children close. Our minds are closed tightly
in the determination that these children shall not be
robbed from us.

The Roman Catholic voice comes as a rumble of thunder; its glance is a shaft of lightning. There is no suggestion that a compromise could ever be made with such.

If, however, that voice is the voice of God, as it claims . . .
if all eternity is here at stake . . .

But, oh! These children in my lap: this habit of sin . . . this
woman . . . this man . . . this fast money . . . this
drunkenness . . .

    These rings in my nose by which I am led around so
    helplessly! They are raising a frightful howl. They
    are screaming plaintively for fresh attentions, new
    gratification, more coddling.

How is it possible to put up with this din . . . to listen
with this din? And yet, where shall I ever find the heart
of bronze needed to silence them?

*   *   *

    A person might easily find himself at the
    Roman Catholic door, but torn with a
    thousand doubts about opening that door
    and going inside. This is a real crisis in
    the life of such a person and can be met
    successfully only by a living and vibrant
    faith . . . the faith which Jesus praised so
    highly when He found it and which He
    lamented when He found it lacking.

It could happen that a man would find himself asking these
questions.

A man is reluctant to empty his heart, and even those who
boast a gargantuan strength to sever their moorings to

earth must compassionate the reluctance in us who are weaker.

A man just doesn't have the strength for murder . . . to stand up suddenly and see the disorderly children he has nourished in his heart fall to their deaths.

It could happen that a man would find himself standing at the door of Christ's Church with many quarrelsome problems on his mind.

Still, as he stands at the Roman Catholic door, he feels an occasional warm breath escaping, and he is cold.

Or he smells the good smell of food, and he is hungry.

He wants that warmth and that food.

He wants to go inside: to be sheltered . . . to be fed.

His hand is trembling on the knob. Lean, white knuckles shine as the hand grips solidly.

In that moment of hesitation, a man might review, and might go back a thousand times over the long journey that has brought him to this door.

He might remember the solemn and demanding voice of Christ:

Who do you say that I am?

. . . and the eager Peter's response:

Thou art the Christ, the Son of the Living God!

. . . or the music in the voice of breathless Andrew as he shouted:

"We have found the Messias!"

"Whoever shall believe in Me, the same shall be saved!"

A man might remember Christ's answer to the question of the Baptist:

"The blind see, the lame walk, the lepers are cleansed, the deaf hear, the dead rise, and the poor have the gospel preached to them."

At Capharnaum: "Arise, take up thy pallet and go to thy house.'"

At Naim: "Young man, I say to thee arise!"

At Bethany: "Lazarus, come forth!"

A man might go back over the tremendous significance of a cross against the sky and an empty tomb.

Over and above these claims, these proofs, he might remember:

> "Thou art Peter, and upon this rock I shall build My Church!"
>
> "The Church of the living God . . . the pillar and mainstay of truth!"
>
> "He who hears you hears Me."
>
> "I will be with you all days, even to the consummation of the world."

*   *   *

All these things might be going through the mind of a man as he stands in the shadow of the Roman Catholic Church.

Behind and beyond that door of separation: a great cumulation of significant history . . . a growth and a greatness of more than human structure . . . From Peter to Pius an unbroken chain of leaders: men who have stood at the helm of the ark, two hundred and sixty-two human representatives of the divine Christ . . . Nineteen hundred years of stability: the same claims, the same faith, the same beliefs . . . and all the while: an unexhausted source of benefit for the whole world.

This — the man thinks — is not the work of an impostor.

This is not a bubble that will someday suddenly burst.

This door — the man thinks — is God's door.

> A turning of this knob and one all-important step and I shall be in God's house.

But in the second between the thinking and the doing: doubt.

What will people say? My parents, my children, or my wife?

Will those I love punish my convictions and my courage
with a "human exile"?

This step I contemplate is permanent . . . Faith which
proceeds only on a money-back guarantee is unaccept-
able. God wants more than this of me.

Do I have the heart and the hands for this sacrifice?

The mind fills up with these doubts.

Faith in the journey and faith that this is the destiny begin
now to lose balance, and struggle sets in.

There is a definite sensation of sinking — sinking right here
at the very door of survival.

Sinking . . . because doubt has been admitted.

The doubt of what will be said, the doubt that my weakness and my habits will cripple my good will and good
intentions . . . the terrifying doubt that if I enter beyond
that door:

I will be lonely.

My strong legs — those which carried me here — are now
weak.

My heart is a rattling thing inside of me.

I am abandoned and I am sinking.

*   *   *

> Conclusion: The answer to doubt and
> indecision as learned from the incident
> of Christ's walking upon the waters of
> Genesareth.

St. Matthew tells us of the time that Jesus had fed five
thousand people. He had sent the disciples to cross the
sea of Galilee before Him, so that He could retire into
the mountains to pray. "But in the fourth watch of the
night He came to them, walking upon the sea. And they,
seeing Him walking upon the sea, were greatly alarmed,
and exclaimed, 'It is a ghost!' And they cried out for

fear. Then Jesus immediately spoke to them, saying,
'Take courage; it is I, do not be afraid.'

"But Peter answered Him and said, 'Lord, if it is Thou,
bid me come to Thee over the water.'

"And He said, 'Come!' "

Sometime in the darkness and silence of the night, this
night of our earthly life, when our eyes are held and our
minds must work things out with great labor, the invitation is given to every man.

"Come!" The voice of Christ says it to the human heart.

It is night . . . the darkness and the tempest and uncertainty
are all about; there is only one anchor:

"Come!"

"Come," Christ says, "come to Me, you who labor and are
burdened, and I will give you rest."

The hands of Christ, the almighty hands of God, go out
to the world! They are the compassionate hands that gave
so much comfort to the sick and the suffering in Galilee.

"Come! Come into the sacred shelter of My Church. Come
into My house and under My roof. Be among My children. Share the light and the warmth of My hearth's
fire, the fire of My Heart.

"Come! Come with a large heart, filled with faith in Me.
Come with a sure trust that it is My voice which brings
you here, that it is really to Me that you are coming."

"Then Peter got out of the boat, and walked on the water
to come to Jesus. But seeing the wind was strong, he
was afraid; and as he began to sink he cried out, saying,
'Lord, save me!' "

Lord, save me . . . save me from the fear that grips me in
this dark night when the wind begins to whip up the
churning sea about me and inside me.

Save me from this fear which challenges my faith, for faith
alone can keep me from sinking.

Save me from the fears that turn my blood to water, as I

think of taking this step out over the water, this step
into the house which You have built.

Save me from the human respect of wondering what people
will think or say, from the fear of petty gossip and prejudice, from the fear of becoming an exile, from the fear
of my own frailty.

Lord, save me from these fears which prevent me from
coming to You. Do not let them harass my heart or hold
back my feet from this step into the warmth and the
light.

"And Jesus at once stretched forth His hand and took hold
of him, saying, to him, 'O thou of little faith, why didst
thou doubt?' And when they got into the boat, the wind
fell. But they who were in the boat came and worshipped
Him, saying:

'Truly Thou art the Son of God.' "

And the man struggling with decision finds those immortal
words of profession in Jesus taste sweet on his lips; he
feels the comfort of them in his heart.

I do not know the course of the road I have taken . . .
Perhaps I have followed a star that shone in the nightly
sky . . . Perhaps it has been a piper's sweet melody that
has led me here. It is unimportant.

The important thing is that I am here.

I know whom I have loved.

"Thou art the Christ, the Son of the living God!"

*   *   *

EPILOGUE

O stranger at my door, how long have You been
waiting there?

What have I been doing that I did not see You there?

How long have my eyes been sightless or my heart a
coward?

Why have I not put my hands into Yours until now?

Has the door between us been my misery or malice,
or have You waited until now to knock?

Has my whole life until now been one prolonged
wintertime because my door has been bolted?

Will You be able to forgive . . . to excuse this rudeness?

*   *   *

The anxious murmurs fall into silence, and the warm voice
of the eternal stranger says only one thing to the anxious
heart of the man:

"Come!"